McGraw-Hill Education

500
ACT Math Questions

to Know by Test Day

D0973390

Also in McGraw-Hill Education 500 Questions Series

ıcation

500
ACT Math Questions
to Know by Test Day

Second Edition

Anaxos, Inc.

New York   Chicago   San Francisco   Athens   London   Madrid
Mexico City   Milan   New Delhi   Singapore   Sydney   Toronto

1 2 3 4 5 6 7 8 9   QFR   22 21 20 19 18

ISBN   978-1-260-10834-7
MHID   1-260-10834-1

e-ISBN   978-1-260-10835-4
e-MHID   1-260-10835-X

ACT is a registered trademark of ACT, Inc., which was not involved in the production of, and does not endorse, this product.

Interior illustrations by Cenveo

McGraw-Hill Education products are available at special quantity discounts to use as premiums and sales promotions or for use in corporate training programs. To contact a representative, please visit the Contact Us pages at www.mhprofessional.com.

CONTENTS

INTRODUCTION

Congratulations! You've taken a big step toward ACT success by purchasing *McGraw-Hill Education 500 ACT Math Questions to Know by Test Day*. We are here to help you take the next step and score high on your ACT exam so you can get into the college or university of your choice!

This book gives you 500 ACT-style multiple-choice questions that cover all the most essential math material. Each question is clearly explained in the answer key. The questions will give you valuable independent practice to supplement your regular textbook and the ground you have already covered in your math class.

This book and the others in the series were written by expert teachers who know the ACT inside and out and can identify crucial information as well as the kinds of questions that are most likely to appear on the exam.

This edition of *McGraw-Hill Education 500 ACT Math Questions to Know by Test Day*, reflects the changes in the ACT Math test instituted in 2017 and includes many new questions. The content is divided into two main categories. The first category is "Integrating Essential Skills," which constitutes 40 percent to 43 percent of the test. This category addresses content typically learned before eighth grade including basic geometry, proportions, rates, and expression of numbers in different ways. The second category is "Preparing for Higher Math," which constitutes 57 percent to 60 percent of the test. This category addresses content typically learned in high school, including algebra, number and quantity, functions, advanced geometry, trigonometry, statistics, and probability. Overlapping both these categories are mathematical modeling problems that involve producing, interpreting, understanding, evaluating, and improving models. Modeling problems in this book are identified with the (MODELING) icon after the problem number.

You might be the kind of student who needs to study extra a few weeks before the exam for a final review. Or you might be the kind of student who puts off preparing until the last minute before the exam. No matter what your preparation style, you will benefit from reviewing these 500 questions, which closely parallel the content, format, and degree of difficulty of the math questions on the actual ACT exam. These questions and the explanations in the answer key are the ideal last-minute study tool for those final weeks before the test.

If you practice with all the questions and answers in this book, we are certain you will build the skills and confidence needed to excel on the ACT. Good luck!

—The Editors of McGraw-Hill Education

McGraw-Hill Education

500
ACT Math Questions

to Know by Test Day

Integrating Essential Skills: Rates, Percentages, and Proportional Relationships

Use the following table to answer questions 1 and 2. It shows the class level of the 500 students at Greenville High School.

Class	Number of Students
Freshmen	125
Sophomores	80
Juniors	175
Seniors	120

1. What percentage of students at Greenville High School are seniors?
    (A) 12%
    (B) 14%
    (C) 24%
    (D) 40%
    (E) 75%

MODELING

2. If the fraction of students who are freshmen is represented using a circle graph (pie chart), what should be the measure (in degrees) of the central angle of that portion of the graph?
    (A) 12
    (B) 25
    (C) 40
    (D) 65
    (E) 90

3. The following chart represents the final course grades for students in two math classes. What fraction of students in the courses received a final course grade of A or B?

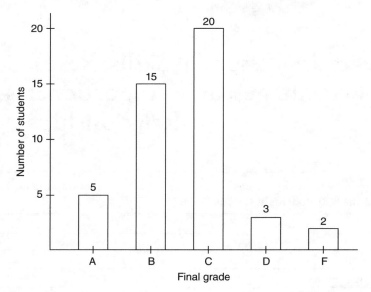

(A) $\dfrac{1}{9}$

(B) $\dfrac{2}{9}$

(C) $\dfrac{3}{9}$

(D) $\dfrac{4}{9}$

(E) $\dfrac{5}{9}$

MODELING 4. The following circle graph represents the distribution of students in a local high school. If there are 1000 total students in the high school, how many more are 9th graders than 11th graders?

Distribution of students by grade level

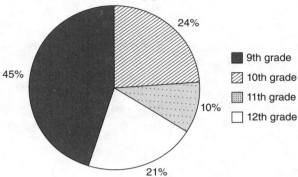

- 9th grade
- 10th grade
- 11th grade
- 12th grade

(A) 500
(B) 450
(C) 350
(D) 120
(E) 100

MODELING 5. A factory can produce 100 bracelets every 15 minutes. How many bracelets can the factory produce in three and a half hours?

(A) 300
(B) 350
(C) 550
(D) 1400
(E) 5250

MODELING 6. A cellular phone service contract requires customers to pay $45.00 a month for basic service in addition to $0.15 for each text message. If a customer's bill is $61.50, how many text messages did the customer send?

(A) 10
(B) 110
(C) 410
(D) 510
(E) 710

7. The ratio of x to y is 5 to 12. If x is 45, what is the value of y?
   (A) 38
   (B) 52
   (C) 60
   (D) 84
   (E) 108

8. If a vehicle is moving at a constant speed of 60 miles per hour, how many miles will it travel in 1 hour and 20 minutes?
   (A) 60
   (B) 65
   (C) 80
   (D) 90
   (E) 105

9. If M% of 135 is 54, then $M =$
   (A) 2.5
   (B) 4
   (C) 25
   (D) 40
   (E) 81

10. In a large company, the ratio of full-time to part-time employees is 3:2. If there are 800 total employees, how many are part-time?
    (A) 260
    (B) 320
    (C) 400
    (D) 480
    (E) 530

11. If the length of one side of a square is increased by 20%, then the perimeter will increase by
    (A) 5%
    (B) 10%
    (C) 20%
    (D) 40%
    (E) 80%

12. If 5% of x is y and 25% of y is z, then how many times larger than z is x?
    (A) 4
    (B) 30
    (C) 80
    (D) 95
    (E) 125

MODELING **13.** A special garden design requires that the garden have three distinct square sections whose areas follow the ratio 2:3:5. If such a garden is designed to have a total area of 1550 square feet, then what would be the area of the smallest section in square feet?

(A) 155
(B) 250
(C) 300
(D) 500
(E) 750

14. In the following figure, triangles *ABC* and *DEF* are similar. What is the value of *x*?

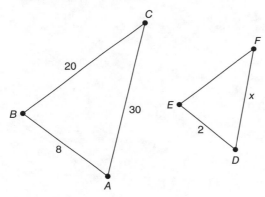

(A) 5.0
(B) 7.5
(C) 15.0
(D) 24.0
(E) 36.5

15. If *a* is directly proportional to $\dfrac{b}{2}$ and *a* = 1 when *b* = 10, then what is the value of *a* when *b* = 35?

(A) $\dfrac{1}{7}$

(B) $\dfrac{1}{5}$

(C) $\dfrac{2}{9}$

(D) $\dfrac{9}{4}$

(E) $\dfrac{7}{2}$

16. If 80% of $x + 1$ is 2, then $x =$
   (A) 0.975
   (B) 1.25
   (C) 1.5
   (D) 4
   (E) 5.1

MODELING **17.** Greg can read w words a minute. How many minutes will it take Greg to read an n-page document if each page contains 500 words?

   (A) $\dfrac{500n}{w}$

   (B) $\dfrac{500w}{n}$

   (C) $500nw$
   (D) $500(n + w)$
   (E) $500n + w$

18. Which of the following represents $\dfrac{1}{2}$ of $\dfrac{1}{20}$?
   (A) 0.000025
   (B) 0.00025
   (C) 0.0025
   (D) 0.025
   (E) 0.25

19. In an election with two parties, Party A won 54% of the votes. If Party B received 874 votes, how many votes were cast in total?
   (A) 400
   (B) 472
   (C) 1619
   (D) 1900
   (E) 2102

20. Each side of square A has a length of 3 meters, while each side of square B has a length of 9 meters. What is the ratio of the area of square A to the area of square B?
   (A) 1:1
   (B) 1:3
   (C) 1:6
   (D) 1:9
   (E) 1:12

21. The ratio of the lengths of each of the sides of a triangle is 4:12:14. If the shortest side has a length of 2 feet, what is the perimeter of the triangle in feet?

    (A) 15
    (B) 24
    (C) 34
    (D) 57
    (E) 68

22. In a college with 14,000 students, 490 are majoring in mathematics. What percentage of the student body does the number of math majors represent?

    (A) 0.0035%
    (B) 0.035%
    (C) 0.35%
    (D) 3.5%
    (E) 35%

23. In the following figure, the ratio of the lengths of AB to BC of rectangle $ABCF$ is 2:3, and C is the midpoint of DF. If $AF = FE$, what is the area of triangle DEF?

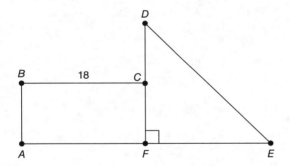

    (A) 12
    (B) 28
    (C) 54
    (D) 108
    (E) 216

24. In the following figure, rectangles *ABCD* and *EFGD* are similar. What is the perimeter of *EFGD*?

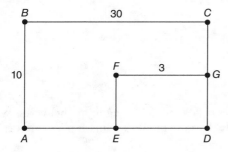

(A) 4
(B) 8
(C) 26
(D) 30
(E) 40

25. If *x* is inversely proportional to *y* and *x* = 12 when *y* = 48, then what is the value of *x* when *y* = 12?

(A) 2
(B) 3
(C) 6
(D) 12
(E) 14

26. If 80% of a number is 122, what is 40% of the number?

(A) 48.8
(B) 61.0
(C) 73.2
(D) 83.0
(E) 244.0

27. A factory's quality assurance specialist can inspect 28 hard drives in 40 minutes. How many minutes will it take the specialist to inspect 196 hard drives?

(A) 47
(B) 49
(C) 89
(D) 137
(E) 280

28. If the ratio of A to B is 3:8 and the ratio of B to C is 1:6, what is the ratio of A to C?

(A) 1:2

(B) 1:14

(C) 1:16

(D) 1:24

(E) 1:48

29. A $154.99 graphing calculator can be purchased with a coupon that gives a 15% discount. What is the price of the calculator if it is purchased with the coupon?

(A) $23.25

(B) $68.47

(C) $131.74

(D) $139.99

(E) $152.67

30. The length of a rectangle is 40% larger than its width. If the area of the rectangle is 140 square feet, what is the width of the rectangle in feet?

(A) 10

(B) 22

(C) 35

(D) 56

(E) 64

31. For $x > 0$, which of the following represents $x\%$ of $\dfrac{3}{4}$?

(A) $\dfrac{3x}{40}$

(B) $\dfrac{3x}{400}$

(C) $\dfrac{3}{400x}$

(D) $\dfrac{1}{28}$

(E) $\dfrac{30x}{4}$

32. What is $\frac{1}{4}$ % of $\frac{1}{4}$?

  (A) 0.000250
  (B) 0.000625
  (C) 0.0025
  (D) 0.0050
  (E) 1

 33. The following table represents the percentages of employees in each of four possible classifications at a certain company. If there are no other possible classifications, what is the value of x?

Classification	Percentage
Part-time	35%
Full-time, hourly	20%
Full-time, salary	24%
Full-time, salary and bonus	x%

  (A) 1
  (B) 21
  (C) 44
  (D) 79
  (E) 65

34. If the ratio of x to y is 1:6, what is the difference between y and x when $x = 12$?

  (A) 5
  (B) 12
  (C) 17
  (D) 60
  (E) 72

35. In the following figure, the ratio of x to y is 1:4. What is the ratio of the area of the triangle with base x to the area of the triangle with base $x + y$?

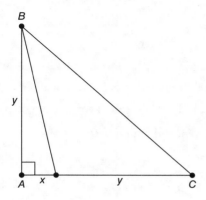

(A) 1:2
(B) 1:4
(C) 1:5
(D) 1:7
(E) Cannot be determined

36. Rectangles $ABCD$ and $PQRS$ in the following figure are similar. What is the value of x?

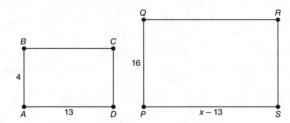

(A) 13
(B) 25
(C) 38
(D) 52
(E) 65

37. If 95% of $3x$ is 39.9, what is the value of x?

(A) 10
(B) 14
(C) 38
(D) 42
(E) 58

38. The circles in the following figure are centered at points O and P, respectively. If $\dfrac{AB}{CD} = 3$, what is the ratio of the area of the circle centered at point O to the area of the circle centered at point P?

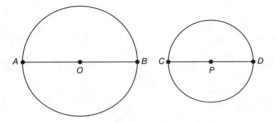

(A) 3:1
(B) 3:2
(C) 6:1
(D) 9:1
(E) 9:2

39. The number representing the length of one side of a square is 20% as large as the number representing its area. What is the perimeter of this square?

(A) 5
(B) 15
(C) 20
(D) 34
(E) 60

40. If the ratio of x to y is 2:5, and y is always 30% of z, then for all possible nonzero values of x, y, and z, $\dfrac{x}{z} =$

(A) $\dfrac{1}{12}$

(B) $\dfrac{3}{25}$

(C) $\dfrac{2}{3}$

(D) $\dfrac{5}{6}$

(E) $\dfrac{3}{4}$

41. If $\dfrac{x}{50} \times 280 = 112$, then $x\%$ of 280 is

(A) 23
(B) 56
(C) 102
(D) 188
(E) 224

42. The triangles in the following figure are similar. In terms of x, what is the perimeter of triangle *DEF*?

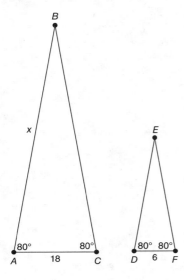

(A) $\dfrac{x}{6}+6$

(B) $\dfrac{x}{3}+6$

(C) $\dfrac{2x}{3}+6$

(D) $2x+6$

(E) $6x+6$

43. A weather station reported that 90% of the days in a 30-day period had measurable snowfall. How many of these days received measurable snowfall?

(A) 3
(B) 12
(C) 18
(D) 27
(E) 29

44. Triangle A and triangle B are equilateral triangles such that the ratio of the length of one side of triangle A to the length of one side of triangle B is 6 to 7. If the perimeter of triangle A is 9, what is the length of a single side of triangle B?

(A) $\dfrac{2}{3}$

(B) $\dfrac{7}{2}$

(C) 12

(D) 18

(E) 21

45. In the following figure, $ABCD$ is a rectangle such that $\dfrac{x}{y} = \dfrac{1}{5}$. If the area of $ABPQ$ is 12, what is the area of $ABCD$?

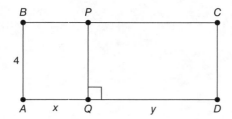

(A) 32

(B) 56

(C) 60

(D) 72

(E) 112

46. The ratio of x to y is 2 to 3. If the sum of x and y is 125, what is the value of x?

(A) 15

(B) 25

(C) 50

(D) 75

(E) 100

47. Which of the following represents 0.2% of $\frac{1}{5}$?

(A) $\dfrac{1}{25,000}$

(B) $\dfrac{1}{2500}$

(C) $\dfrac{1}{250}$

(D) $\dfrac{1}{25}$

(E) $\dfrac{1}{10}$

48. For any circle with radius $r > 0$, what is the ratio of the length of its radius to its area?

(A) $1 : \pi$

(B) $1 : 2\pi$

(C) $1 : \pi r$

(D) $1 : 2\pi r$

(E) $1 : \pi r^2$

MODELING **49.** Every student enrolled in a science course is either a physics major or a biology major. If the ratio of physics majors to biology majors is 3 to 1 and there are 21 physics majors enrolled, how many biology majors are enrolled in the course?

(A) 7
(B) 15
(C) 23
(D) 45
(E) 63

50. Suppose that m is inversely proportional to n and that $m = \dfrac{1}{2}$ when $n = 6$. If $n = \dfrac{2}{3}$, what is the value of m?

(A) $\dfrac{1}{6}$

(B) 2
(C) 3

(D) $\dfrac{9}{2}$

(E) 6

51. The value of a positive number x is 30% of the value of a positive number y. If 20% of y is 8, what is the value of x?

(A) 10
(B) 12
(C) 16
(D) 40
(E) 70

52. If y is directly proportional to x and if $y = 6$ when $x = \dfrac{1}{4}$, then which of the following equations describes the relationship between x and y?

(A) $y = \dfrac{1}{4}x$

(B) $y = \dfrac{3}{2}x$

(C) $y = \dfrac{23}{4}x$

(D) $y = 6x$

(E) $y = 24x$

53. A rectangle has sides of length x and $x + 1$, where x is a positive number. If the area of the rectangle is 12, then which of the following is equivalent to the ratio of x to $x + 1$?

(A) 1:6
(B) 1:4
(C) 1:3
(D) 2:3
(E) 3:4

54. If the length of one side of a square is 28% of 50, then the area of the square is equal to

(A) 70
(B) 84
(C) 140
(D) 196
(E) 289

55. If q% of 30 is 21, then $q =$
(A) 50
(B) 60
(C) 70
(D) 80
(E) 90

MODELING **56.** This week, the price of a plane ticket is $436.00. Over the next three weeks, suppose the price of the ticket rises 5% in the first week, falls 10% the next week, and then rises 20% in the third week. To the nearest cent, what is the cost of the plane ticket in three weeks?
(A) $412.02
(B) $457.80
(C) $494.42
(D) $501.40
(E) $523.20

57. Of 600 items in a storage closet, 40% are pens or pencils, 10% are first-aid items, and 5% are notebooks. How many items in the storage closet have not been described?
(A) 45
(B) 60
(C) 240
(D) 270
(E) 300

58. A number a is four times as large as half of a number b. If a and b are nonzero, what percent of a is b?
(A) 20%
(B) 25%
(C) 50%
(D) 100%
(E) 400%

MODELING **59.** A particle can move along the x-axis of the (x, y) coordinate plane at the rate of 3 units every $\dfrac{1}{2}$ hour. If the particle begins at the origin and moves in the positive x direction, at what point will it be in $2\dfrac{1}{4}$ hours?

(A) $\left(\dfrac{9}{8}, 0\right)$

(B) $\left(\dfrac{27}{8}, 0\right)$

(C) $\left(\dfrac{9}{2}, 0\right)$

(D) $\left(\dfrac{27}{4}, 0\right)$

(E) $\left(\dfrac{27}{2}, 0\right)$

60. In the following figure, the ratio of x to y is 1:4. What is the value of x?

$2\sqrt{17}$

y

x

(A) 1
(B) 2
(C) 8
(D) 10
(E) 13

61. Points A, B, and C in the following figure are collinear. If the ratio of m to n is 2:3, what is the value of n in degrees?

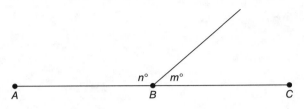

    (A) 36
    (B) 94
    (C) 108
    (D) 120
    (E) 170

62. If, for nonzero values of m, n, and x, $\dfrac{m}{n} = \dfrac{4}{9}$ and $\dfrac{n}{x} = \dfrac{4}{3}$, then $\dfrac{m}{x} =$

    (A) $\dfrac{1}{27}$

    (B) $\dfrac{1}{3}$

    (C) $\dfrac{16}{27}$

    (D) $\dfrac{31}{12}$

    (E) $\dfrac{16}{3}$

63. If $\dfrac{2}{5}\%$ of x is 10, then $\dfrac{1}{5}\%$ of x must equal

    (A) 5
    (B) 10
    (C) 20
    (D) 25
    (E) 30

64. Every 6 minutes, a red LED flashes to indicate that a machine is operating correctly. If the machine operates correctly for 800 minutes, how many times will the LED flash?

(A) 133
(B) 134
(C) 135
(D) 136
(E) 137

65. In the following figure, $AC = CE = 4$, C is the midpoint of BD, and $ABDE$ is a rectangle. What is the ratio of the area of triangle ACE to the area of triangle ABC?

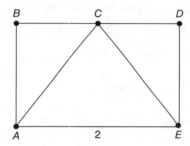

(A) 2:1
(B) 4:1
(C) 8:1
(D) 10:1
(E) 15:1

66. If $\frac{1}{2}\%$ of $\frac{x}{14}$ is $\frac{1}{4}$, then $x =$

(A) 7
(B) 70
(C) 700
(D) 7000
(E) 70,000

MODELING **67.** A tenant's monthly rent of $675 will be increased by 3% every year. To the nearest cent, what will be the tenant's monthly rent in 3 years?

(A) $695.25
(B) $735.75
(C) $737.59
(D) $781.02
(E) $794.66

68. If $\dfrac{2x}{y} = \dfrac{4}{7}$, then how many times larger than x is y?

(A) $\dfrac{7}{4}$

(B) $\dfrac{7}{2}$

(C) 4

(D) 14

(E) 28

69. A student's parking pass costs $45 per semester this year but last year cost only $38 per semester. To the nearest tenth of a percent, by what percentage has the price of a parking pass increased?

(A) 15.6%

(B) 18.4%

(C) 24.3%

(D) 28.6%

(E) 31.1%

MODELING **70.** For the first two hours he is at work, Harrison files 14 folders each hour. For the remainder of his workday, he files 22 folders every hour. Which of the following best models the number of folders (F) Harrison files if he works a total of H hours during his workday?

(A) F = 14 + 22H

(B) F = 28 + 22H

(C) F = 22 + 28H

(D) F = 28 + 22 (H − 2)

(E) F = 22 + 28 (H − 2)

CHAPTER 2

Integrating Essential Skills: Basic Geometry

Use the following information to answer questions 71–72.

The front of a house, shown in the unscaled diagram below, was damaged in a hailstorm. New wood trim is needed around the perimeter of the house as well as around the door and window, but trim is not needed along the base of the house and door. The wall and the trim also need 2 fresh coats of paint. The window is a square with 4-foot sides, and the door is 6 feet tall and 3 feet wide.

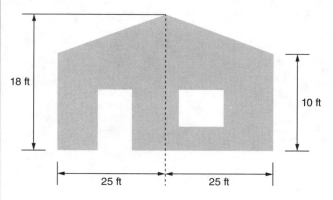

18 ft

10 ft

25 ft   25 ft

MODELING

71. House trim costs $0.50 per foot. How much money, to the nearest dollar, must be budgeted to replace the trim?

(A) $50

(B) $52

(C) $72

(D) $75

(E) $83

MODELING **72.** One gallon of paint covers about 400 square feet. How many gallons of paint are needed for the project detailed above?

(A) 2
(B) 3
(C) 4
(D) 5
(E) 6

73. If the coordinates of the point X have the same sign, then X must be located in which of the four quadrants seen in the following figure?

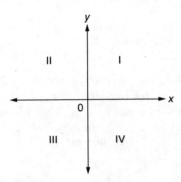

(A) I only
(B) II only
(C) I and II only
(D) I and III only
(E) III and IV only

74. As shown in the following figure, the angle between lines m and ℓ is 90 degrees. What must the product of their slopes equal?

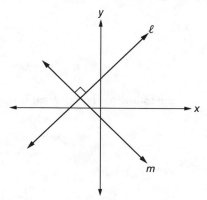

(A) −2
(B) −1
(C) 0
(D) 1
(E) Cannot be determined

75. Which of the following statements must be true regarding the line graphed in the following figure?

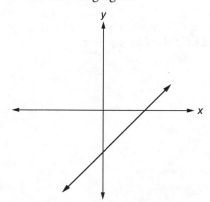

I. The slope of the line is positive.
II. The x-intercept of the line is negative.
III. The y-intercept of the line is positive.

(A) I only
(B) II only
(C) III only
(D) I and II only
(E) I, II, and III

76. A rectangle has a width of 5 meters and a length of 14 meters. If a similar rectangle has a width of 15 meters, what is its perimeter, in meters?

(A) 42
(B) 58
(C) 60
(D) 78
(E) 114

77. Lines AB and ℓ intersect at point C in the following figure. What is the value of x in degrees?

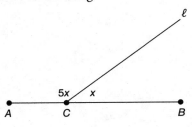

(A) 20
(B) 30
(C) 45
(D) 55
(E) 80

78. In the following figure, lines AB and CD intersect at a point P. If $\angle APD = 80°$, what is the measure of $\angle APC$ in degrees?

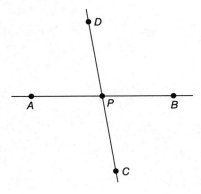

(A) 10
(B) 100
(C) 170
(D) 200
(E) 280

79. Line ℓ is a transversal of the parallel lines m and n as shown in the figure. The measures of two angles are given in terms of x and y. What is the value of x in degrees?

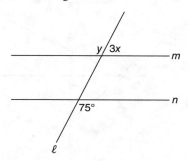

(A) 25
(B) 30
(C) 35
(D) 50
(E) 75

80. If a line in the (x, y) coordinate plane has x-intercept $(x, 0)$ and y-intercept $(0, y)$ such that $x > y$, which of the following could be a graph of the line?

(A)
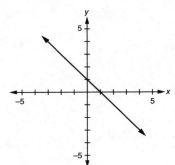

(B)
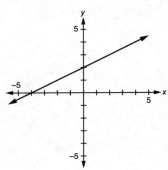

(C)
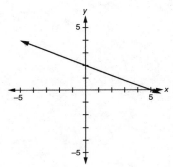

(D)
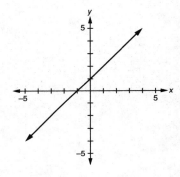

(E)
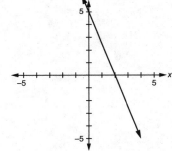

81. If lines AB and CD are perpendicular and intersect at point P, what is the measure of $\angle APB$ in degrees?

(A) 30
(B) 45
(C) 60
(D) 90
(E) 180

82. In the following figure, the circle centered at point P has a radius of 2, and AB is parallel to the x-axis. If the line segments AB and DC are both diameters such that A has coordinates $(1, 4)$, what are the coordinates of point D?

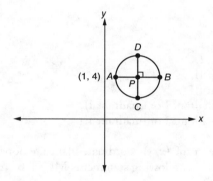

(A) $(-1, 4)$
(B) $(1, 2)$
(C) $(3, 4)$
(D) $(3, 6)$
(E) $(5, 4)$

83. The coordinates of a point P are (x, y) such that $xy > 0$. Given the four quadrants of the (x, y) coordinate plane shown, which of the following statements MUST be true?

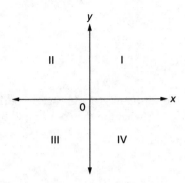

(A) Point P must lie in quadrant I.
(B) Point P must lie in quadrant II.
(C) Point P must lie in quadrant III.
(D) Point P must lie in either quadrant I or quadrant II.
(E) Point P must lie in either quadrant I or quadrant III.

84. If the x- and y-intercepts of a line in the (x, y) coordinate plane are nonzero and share the same sign, which of the following statements MUST be true?

(A) The slope of the line is negative.
(B) The slope of the line is positive.
(C) The slope of the line is zero.
(D) The slope of the line is undefined.
(E) The slope of the line is nonzero and defined.

85. Which of the following lines has a slope of zero?

(A)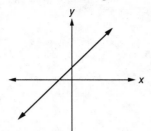

(B)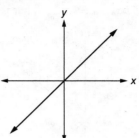

(C)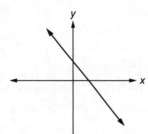

(D)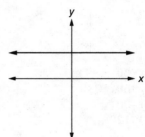

(E)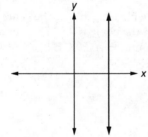

86. The points A (1, 0), B (1, 8), and C (5, 0) form a triangle in the (x, y) coordinate plane. In coordinate units, what is the area of triangle ABC?

(A) 3
(B) 12
(C) 16
(D) 32
(E) 40

87. In the following figure, lines m, n, and ℓ intersect to form angles with the indicated measures. What is the value of $x + y + z$?

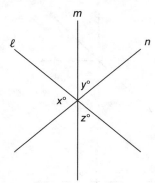

    (A) 30
    (B) 60
    (C) 90
    (D) 120
    (E) 180

88. A circle is drawn in the (x, y) coordinate plane such that the center of the circle is the point $(0, 7)$. If the radius of the circle is 2, then each of the following points lies on the circle's circumference EXCEPT

    (A) $(-2, 7)$
    (B) $(0, 9)$
    (C) $(0, 5)$
    (D) $(1, 7)$
    (E) $(2, 7)$

89. Which of the following graphs represents a line with a positive slope and a negative *x*-intercept?

(A)

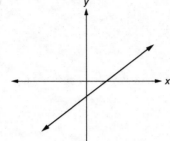

(B)

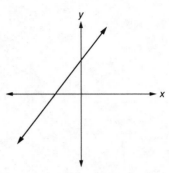

(C)

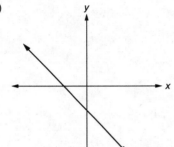

(D)

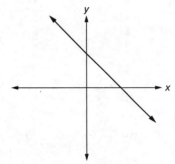

(E)

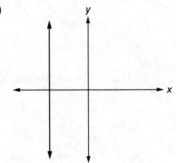

90. For a line in the (x, y) coordinate plane, which of the following statements is always true of the *y*-intercept?

(A) The coordinates are of the form $(c, 0)$ for some number c.
(B) The coordinates are of the form $(0, c)$ for some number c.
(C) If the slope is positive, the *y*-intercept is positive.
(D) The larger the slope, the larger the *y*-intercept.
(E) The origin can never be the *y*-intercept.

91. In the following figure, triangles *ABC* and *DEF* are similar. Which of the following expressions represents the area of *DEF* in terms of *x* and *y*?

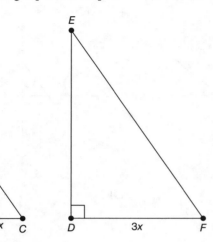

(A) $\dfrac{xy}{2}$

(B) $\dfrac{3xy}{2}$

(C) $3xy$

(D) $\dfrac{9xy}{2}$

(E) $6xy$

92. In the (x, y) coordinate plane, if the point $(x, -5)$ lies on the graph of the line $5y - 2x = -30$, what is the value of x?

(A) -10

(B) -8

(C) $-\dfrac{23}{5}$

(D) $\dfrac{5}{2}$

(E) 15

93. In the following figure, *PR*, *MQ*, and *NQ* are line segments such that ∠*PQM* = ∠*NQR*.

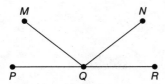

If the measure of ∠*PQM* is half the measure of ∠*MQN*, then the measure of ∠*NQR* is

(A) 35°
(B) 45°
(C) 90°
(D) 100°
(E) 120°

94. If the angle between two perpendicular lines has a measure of $(2x + 2)°$, then $x =$

(A) 44
(B) 45
(C) 89
(D) 90
(E) 91

95. The interior angles of a triangle are *x*, *y*, and *z*. If $x = 45°$ and $y = 90°$, then $z =$

(A) 25°
(B) 35°
(C) 45°
(D) 55°
(E) 65°

96. In inches, what is the perimeter of a rectangle with a width of 4 inches and a length of 10 inches?

(A) 14
(B) 18
(C) 28
(D) 40
(E) 160

97. In the following figure, the area of square *ABCD* is 16 square units. What is the circumference of the circle centered at point *B*?

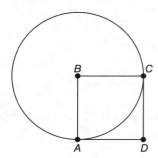

(A) 2π

(B) 4π

(C) 8π

(D) 16π

(E) 32π

98. The area of a circle is 8π square units. What is the radius of the circle?

(A) $2\sqrt{2}$

(B) 4

(C) $4\sqrt{2}$

(D) 8

(E) 12

99. The length of the shortest side of a triangle is 10 meters, and the length of one of the longer sides is 20 meters. If the two larger angles in the triangle are equal, what is the perimeter of the triangle in meters?

(A) 40

(B) 45

(C) 50

(D) 55

(E) 87

100. The value of a square's area is twice as large as the value of its perimeter. In units, what is the length of one side of the square?

(A) 4

(B) 8

(C) 12

(D) 16

(E) 32

101. The length of the diagonal of a rectangle is 20 feet. If the width of the rectangle is 12 feet, what is its area in square feet?

(A) 28
(B) 144
(C) 192
(D) 256
(E) 400

102. The sides of a triangle have lengths of 3, 3, and 5.2 meters. If one of the smaller angles in the triangle has a measure of 30°, what is the measure of the largest angle?

(A) 60°
(B) 90°
(C) 100°
(D) 120°
(E) 140°

103. Each of the smallest angles in a parallelogram is 50°. Which of the following is the measure of each of largest angles in the parallelogram?

(A) 40°
(B) 80°
(C) 130°
(D) 260°
(E) 310°

104. The circles in the following figure are centered at point *O*. In square centimeters, what is the area of the shaded region?

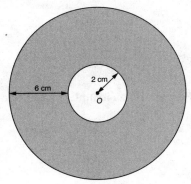

(A) 15π
(B) 21π
(C) 32π
(D) 35π
(E) 60π

105. Given the trapezoid in the following figure, what is the value of x?

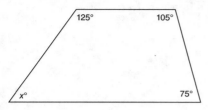

(A) 55
(B) 65
(C) 75
(D) 95
(E) 105

106. In the following figure, the points A, C, and D lie along the same line, and ABC is a triangle with sides of the indicated length. If the measure of angle CAB is 85°, what is the measure of angle BCD in degrees?

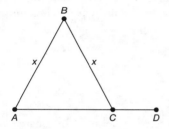

(A) 85
(B) 95
(C) 105
(D) 115
(E) 120

107. In square units, what is the area of a circle with a circumference of 6π?

(A) 3π
(B) 6π
(C) 9π
(D) 12π
(E) 36π

108. In the following figure, the square *ABCD* is a single side of a cube with a volume of 8 cubic inches. In inches, what is the length of the line *BD*?

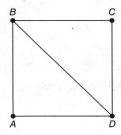

(A) 1
(B) $\sqrt{2}$
(C) 2
(D) $2\sqrt{2}$
(E) 4

109. Given the right triangle in the following figure, what is the value of *x*?

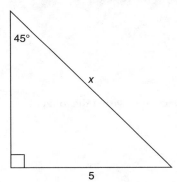

(A) $2\sqrt{2}$

(B) $5\sqrt{2}$

(C) $\sqrt{5}$

(D) $2\sqrt{5}$

(E) $\sqrt{10}$

110. In inches, what is the radius of a sphere with a volume of 36π?

(A) 1
(B) 3
(C) 6
(D) 9
(E) 12

111. In the following figure, $AB = BC = AC$, and BD bisects the angle ABC. What is the value of x?

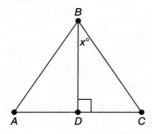

(A) 15
(B) 20
(C) 30
(D) 45
(E) 60

112. In square meters, what is the area of a rectangle with a diagonal of 25 meters and a width of 15 meters?

(A) 200
(B) 250
(C) 275
(D) 300
(E) 375

113. In the following figure, *ABCD* is a parallelogram such that *AB* has a length of 3 centimeters and *BC* has a length of 7 centimeters. What is the perimeter of *ABCD*?

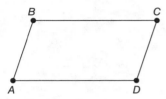

    (A) 10
    (B) 20
    (C) 30
    (D) 40
    (E) 50

114. A rectangular container measuring 4 feet wide, 8 feet long, and 3 feet tall is filled with a 1-foot-deep layer of sand. In cubic feet, what volume of the container remains unfilled?

    (A) 18
    (B) 32
    (C) 42
    (D) 64
    (E) 72

115. Two squares of the same size overlap such that all three of the resulting rectangles shown in the figure have the same area. If the area of the shaded rectangle is 2, what is the area of one of the original squares?

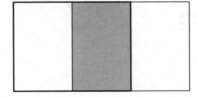

    (A) 2
    (B) 4
    (C) 9
    (D) 16
    (E) 25

MODELING **116.** The following figure represents the dimensions of three rooms of a house that are to be completely carpeted. In total, how many square feet of carpet will be needed?

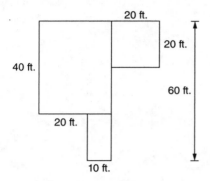

(A) 1200
(B) 1300
(C) 1500
(D) 1700
(E) 1800

117. Triangle *ABC* in the following figure is an isosceles triangle with height *BD*. What is the value of *a*?

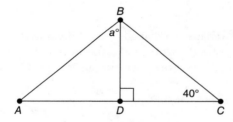

(A) 45
(B) 50
(C) 60
(D) 65
(E) 90

118. The interior angles of a triangle measure $x°$, $(2x)°$, and $(3x)°$. The value of x MUST be

(A) 30
(B) 35
(C) 45
(D) 50
(E) 65

119. In the following figure, the circles centered at points B and D are tangent at the point C, and each circle has an area of 49π. What is the length of the line segment AE?

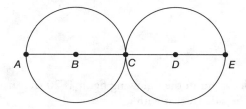

(A) 14
(B) 28
(C) 42
(D) 48
(E) 56

120. If one of the interior angles of a triangle measures $72°$, each of the following pairs could represent the measures of the remaining angles EXCEPT

(A) 58°, 50°
(B) 42°, 66°
(C) 15°, 93°
(D) 87°, 21°
(E) 36°, 73°

121. The length of a rectangle is 5 times its width. If the width is represented by w, which of the following expressions is the perimeter of the rectangle in terms of w?

(A) $5w$
(B) $6w$
(C) $10w$
(D) $12w$
(E) $14w$

122. In the following figure, *FBCE* is a rectangle, while *ABF* and *ECD* are congruent right triangles. What is the area of the quadrilateral *ABCD*?

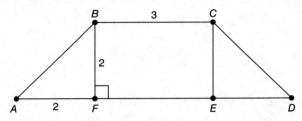

(A) 6
(B) 8
(C) 10
(D) 12
(E) 16

123. The perimeter of the parallelogram in the following figure is 20 feet. In feet, what is the length of the side labeled with an *x*?

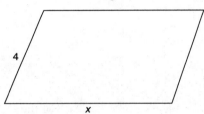

(A) 4
(B) 6
(C) 8
(D) 12
(E) 16

124. A rectangle has an area of 45 square meters and a width of 9 meters. In meters, what is the length of the rectangle?

(A) 5
(B) 7
(C) 14
(D) 27
(E) 36

MODELING **125.** A modern-art piece begins as a special canvas with dimensions shown in the following figure. Initially, the canvas will be painted with a base coat of flat paint. If one tube of the paint can cover four square feet, how many tubes will the artist need in order to apply the base coat?

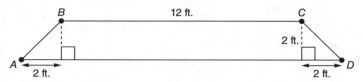

(A) 6
(B) 7
(C) 8
(D) 9
(E) 10

126. A circle has a diameter of length d and an area of A. If the diameter of the circle is tripled, the area of the new circle is B. How many times larger than A is B?

(A) 3
(B) 6
(C) 9
(D) 12
(E) 18

127. When completely filled, a spherical balloon contains exactly $\dfrac{32\pi}{3}$ cubic feet of air. In feet, what is the radius of the balloon when it is completely filled?

(A) 2

(B) $\dfrac{4\sqrt{6}}{3}$

(C) 4

(D) $2\sqrt{6}$

(E) 8

128. In the following figure, the points A, B, C, and D lie along the same line. What is the difference of x and y?

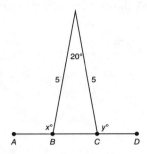

(A) 0
(B) 20
(C) 60
(D) 160
(E) 200

129. In square meters, what is the area of a single face of a cube that has a volume of 125 cubic meters?

(A) $2\sqrt{3}$
(B) 5
(C) $5\sqrt{5}$
(D) 25
(E) 63

130. Which of the following expressions represents the area of a right triangle with legs of lengths x and y?

(A) $\dfrac{xy}{2}$

(B) $\dfrac{x^2 y^2}{2}$

(C) $\dfrac{x+y}{2}$

(D) $\dfrac{x^2 - y^2}{2}$

(E) $\dfrac{\sqrt{x^2 + y^2}}{2}$

131. In the following figure, *ABCD* is a rectangle, and *BD* is one of its diagonals. If the area of the triangle *ABD* is 6 square meters, what is the area of *ABCD* in square meters?

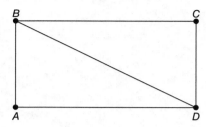

    (A) 3
    (B) 6
    (C) 12
    (D) 18
    (E) 24

132. In feet, what is the perimeter of a square that has an area of 49 square feet?

    (A) 14
    (B) 28
    (C) 56
    (D) 98
    (E) 196

133. In the following figure, *ABCD* is a rectangle, and *PQR* is an equilateral triangle. Given the provided measurements are in inches, what is the area of the rectangle *ABCD* in square inches?

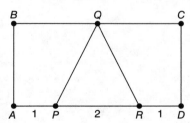

    (A) $\sqrt{3}$

    (B) $2\sqrt{3}$
    (C) 5
    (D) 8
    (E) $4\sqrt{3}$

134. If $x \neq y$, which of the following expressions represents the perimeter of the triangle in the following figure in terms of x and y?

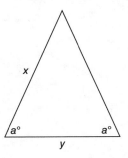

    (A) $x + y$
    (B) $x + y + 2$
    (C) $2x + y$
    (D) $x + 2y$
    (E) $2(x + y)$

135. The parallelogram in the following figure has a perimeter of 32 feet. If x is three times as large as y, what is the value of x in feet?

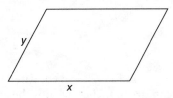

    (A) 2
    (B) 4
    (C) 8
    (D) 12
    (E) 24

136. In the following figure, *ABC* is a triangle such that *M* is the midpoint of *AB* and *N* is the midpoint of *AC*. If the area of triangle *ABC* is 12, what is the length of side *AB*?

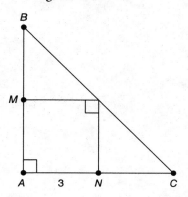

(A) 2
(B) 4
(C) 6
(D) 8
(E) 10

137. The sides of the rhombus *ABCD* in the following figure all have the same length, and the dashed line *AC* is a diagonal of *ABCD*.

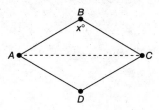

If the measure of $\angle BCD = 60°$, then $x =$

(A) 30
(B) 40
(C) 60
(D) 120
(E) 180

138. A circle is divided into 8 equal sections, as shown in the following figure. What is the value of angle x in degrees?

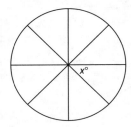

(A) 25
(B) 36
(C) 45
(D) 50
(E) 55

139. Which of the following values represents the circumference of a circle whose radius is $\dfrac{1}{\pi}$?

(A) $\dfrac{1}{2}$
(B) 1
(C) 2
(D) π
(E) 2π

140. If the interior angles of a quadrilateral have measures $x°$, $(2x)°$, $(x + 45)°$, and $(x + 55)°$, then $x =$

(A) 16
(B) 23
(C) 52
(D) 65
(E) 78

Integrating Essential Skills: Average, Median, and Expressing Numbers in Different Ways

MODELING

141. In a small graduate class of five students, Juan's exam score was accidentally deleted from the gradebook. The professor recalls that the exam average was 84%. Which student earned the median exam score?

Student	Exam Score
George	76%
Tamara	88%
Juan	?
Sarita	75%
Alysia	92%

(A) George
(B) Tamara
(C) Juan
(D) Sarita
(E) Alysia

142. What is the greatest common factor of 30, 90, and 130?

(A) 2
(B) 3
(C) 5
(D) 10
(E) 30

143. What is the median of $\sqrt{2}$, 5, $\sqrt{3}$, 1, and $\sqrt{5}$?

    (A) $\sqrt{2}$

    (B) 5

    (C) $\sqrt{3}$

    (D) 1

    (E) $\sqrt{5}$

144. Which of the following is an irrational number?

    (A) $\sqrt{\dfrac{100}{169}}$

    (B) $\sqrt{\dfrac{1}{4}}$

    (C) $\sqrt{16}$

    (D) $\sqrt{81}$

    (E) $\sqrt{99}$

145. Which of the following must be true whenever a, b, and c are integers such that $a < 0$ and $b > c > 0$?

    (A) $a - c > 0$

    (B) $c - b < 0$

    (C) $a + c > 0$

    (D) $-a - c < 0$

    (E) $a + b > 0$

146. What is the largest integer smaller than $\sqrt{50}$?

    (A) 4

    (B) 6

    (C) 7

    (D) 9

    (E) 12

147. The sum of 10 numbers is 250. What is the average of the 10 numbers?

    (A) 25

    (B) 50

    (C) 110

    (D) 125

    (E) 240

148. If m and n are integers, which of the following must be an even integer?

(A) $2mn$

(B) mn

(C) $mn + 2$

(D) $mn - 2$

(E) $3mn$

149. If the equation $|x - a| = |y - a|$ is true, then which of the following must be true?

(A) $|x| = |y|$

(B) $x > a$

(C) $|x + y| \neq 0$

(D) $y < a$

(E) $|-a + y| = |-a + x|$

150. If P is the set of multiples of 2, Q is the set of multiples of 3, and R is the set of multiples of 7, which of the following integers will be in P and Q but not in R?

(A) -54

(B) -50

(C) 42

(D) 100

(E) 252

151. Using the following number line, which pairs of points satisfy the equation $|x - y| < \dfrac{1}{2}$?

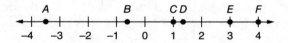

(A) $x = A, y = B$

(B) $x = B, y = C$

(C) $x = C, y = D$

(D) $x = D, y = E$

(E) $x = E, y = F$

152. What is the average of the numbers $\frac{5}{4}$, $\frac{1}{2}$, and $\frac{x}{2}$?

    (A) $\dfrac{2x+7}{12}$

    (B) $\dfrac{4x+9}{12}$

    (C) $\dfrac{x+6}{6}$

    (D) $\dfrac{2x+7}{4}$

    (E) $\dfrac{x+9}{4}$

153. If $3(m + n)$ is even, then which of the following must also be even?

    (A) $m + n$
    (B) m
    (C) n
    (D) $3m$
    (E) $3n + 1$

154. A number is a multiple of both 4 and 9. Which of the following is NOT a possible value of the number?

    (A) −540
    (B) −324
    (C) 126
    (D) 144
    (E) 360

155. There are 45 students signed up for the performance band, while 30 are signed up for the jazz band. If 19 students are signed up for both bands, how many students are signed up for only one of the bands?

    (A) 11
    (B) 16
    (C) 37
    (D) 56
    (E) 75

156. Which of the following inequalities represents the same set as the set graphed on the number line shown?

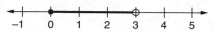

(A) $0 < x < 3$

(B) $0 \le x \le 3$

(C) $-1 < x < 5$

(D) $-1 \le x < 3$

(E) $0 \le x < 3$

157. If the following numbers were ordered from smallest to largest, which would be in the third position?

$$\left(\frac{1}{2}\right)^{-2}, \frac{1}{3}, \sqrt{17}, \pi, \sqrt{3}$$

(A) $\left(\frac{1}{2}\right)^{-2}$

(B) $\dfrac{1}{3}$

(C) $\sqrt{17}$

(D) π

(E) $\sqrt{3}$

158. If p and q are real numbers such that $(pq)^2 = 4$, then which of the following statements must also be true?

(A) $pq > 0$

(B) $pq = 2$

(C) $p > 1$ and $q > 1$

(D) If $p < 0$, then $q > 0$

(E) If $p > 2$, then $q < 2$

159. What is the median of the following set of numbers?
{1, 1, 9, 4, 6, 2}

(A) 1

(B) 2

(C) 3

(D) 4

(E) 6

160. What is the value of $\left|-2x-5\right|-\left|-4+8\right|$ when $x = 7$?

(A) −12
(B) −4
(C) 7
(D) 15
(E) 23

161. For positive integers x and y, $x + y = 21$. What is the smallest possible value of xy?

(A) 10
(B) 20
(C) 38
(D) 54
(E) 110

162. For a real number x, the expression $\dfrac{\sqrt{x}}{5}$ is an integer. Each of the following expression must also be integers EXCEPT

(A) $\left(\dfrac{\sqrt{x}}{5}\right)^2$

(B) $10\sqrt{x}$

(C) $\dfrac{\sqrt{x}}{25}$

(D) $\dfrac{6\sqrt{x}}{5}$

(E) $-\sqrt{x}$

163. What is the value of $\sqrt{48} - \sqrt{27}$?

(A) 0
(B) $\sqrt{2}$
(C) $\sqrt{3}$
(D) $\sqrt{11}$
(E) $\sqrt{21}$

164. Which of the following values of x satisfies the inequality $\sqrt{26} < x < \sqrt{50}$?

(A) 3

(B) 5

(C) 6

(D) 9

(E) 10

165. $-2\left|-1+5\right| =$

(A) -8

(B) -6

(C) 2

(D) 6

(E) 8

166. Which of the following is a rational number?

(A) $\dfrac{\sqrt{2}}{2}$

(B) $\left(\sqrt{2}-2\right)^2$

(C) $\dfrac{\sqrt{100}}{5}$

(D) $\sqrt{3}$

(E) $\left(3+\sqrt{3}\right)^2$

167. If x and y are real numbers such that $0 < x < y^2$, then which of the following inequalities must be true?

(A) $x < y$

(B) $y > 0$

(C) $3x > y^2$

(D) $x < 1$

(E) $x < 3y^2$

168. What is the value of $\sqrt{x+(-x)^2}$ when $x = -1$?

(A) -1

(B) 0

(C) 1

(D) $\sqrt{2}$

(E) $\sqrt{3}$

169. What is the smallest integer larger than $\dfrac{\sqrt{26}}{5}$?

(A) 1
(B) 2
(C) 4
(D) 5
(E) 6

170. Using the following number line, which point satisfies the inequality $\left|-x+1\right| > 4$?

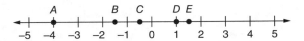

(A) *A*
(B) *B*
(C) *C*
(D) *D*
(E) *E*

171. Suppose that *m* is an even integer and *n* is an odd integer. Which of the following expressions must be an odd integer?

(A) $2(m + n)$
(B) $2(m + n) + 1$
(C) *mn*
(D) $2(mn)$
(E) $3(mn)$

172. Let *P* represent the set of numbers with a factor of 5, and let *Q* represent the set of numbers that are less than 10 but larger than 0. Which of the following numbers is in both sets?

(A) −10
(B) −5
(C) 2
(D) 5
(E) 8

173. What is the least common multiple of 12, 20, and 40?

(A) 60
(B) 120
(C) 480
(D) 800
(E) 9600

174. If p and q are real numbers such that $p > 5$ and $q > 4$, what is the smallest integer larger than the product pq?

(A) 9
(B) 10
(C) 19
(D) 20
(E) 21

175. A number has three prime factors: 2, 3, and 7. Which of the following is a possible value of the number?

(A) 12
(B) 14
(C) 49
(D) 81
(E) 84

MODELING **176.** There are 53 people signed up for a race on an upcoming Saturday, and there are 21 people signed up for a race on an upcoming Sunday. If 12 people signed up for both races, how many people are signed up for only one race?

(A) 9
(B) 41
(C) 50
(D) 62
(E) 74

177. The value of $\dfrac{x+y}{y}$ is an integer when $y = 4$. Which of the following is a possible value of x?

(A) −16
(B) 2
(C) 9
(D) 15
(E) 26

178. If a set is defined as all numbers satisfying a given inequality, then which of the following sets would NOT share any values with the set of values for x satisfying $-1 \le x < 5$?

(A) $-5 \le x < -1$
(B) $-5 < x \le -1$
(C) $0 < x < 5$
(D) $0 < x \le 5$
(E) $0 < x \le 5$

179. Let $x \triangleright y = \dfrac{y}{x}$ for real numbers x and y. For what values of x is the value of $x \triangleright (-1)$ always positive?

(A) $x > 0$
(B) $x < 0$
(C) $x > -1$
(D) $x < 1$
(E) $x > 1$

180. If m is the number of distinct prime factors of 100, what is the value of $3m$?

(A) 3
(B) 6
(C) 9
(D) 12
(E) 15

181. For any real number a, $(6a^5)^2 =$

(A) $12a^7$
(B) $36a^7$
(C) $12a^{10}$
(D) $36a^{10}$
(E) $8a^3$

182. If the average of 12 numbers is m, which of the following expressions represents the average of these 12 numbers and 5?

(A) $m + 5$
(B) $m + 13$
(C) $13m + 5$
(D) $\dfrac{m+5}{13}$
(E) $\dfrac{12m+5}{13}$

183. Using the following number line, which of the following statements must be true?

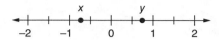

(A) $|x-y|<1$

(B) $|x-y|=1$

(C) $|x-y|>1$

(D) $|x-y|<\dfrac{1}{2}$

(E) $|x-y|=\dfrac{1}{2}$

184. The following table represents the number of town residents who live in each district. If the total number of residents in the town is 650, how many residents live in district 2?

District	Number of Residents
1	147
2	?
3	335
4	98

(A) 42
(B) 70
(C) 315
(D) 503
(E) 552

185. The average of five numbers is 12.4. The average of four of these numbers is 11. What is the value of the fifth number?

(A) 1.4
(B) 17.0
(C) 18.0
(D) 44.0
(E) 62.0

186. Which of the following values of x satisfies the inequality $\frac{3}{2} < x < \frac{5}{2}$?

(A) $\dfrac{\sqrt{9}}{2}$

(B) $\dfrac{\sqrt{20}}{2}$

(C) $\dfrac{\sqrt{25}}{2}$

(D) $\dfrac{\sqrt{29}}{2}$

(E) $\dfrac{\sqrt{31}}{2}$

187. If $xy^2 < 0$, then which of the following statements must be true?

(A) The value of x is negative, while the value of y is positive or negative.
(B) The value of y is negative, while the value of x is positive or negative.
(C) The sign of x must be the same as the sign of y.
(D) The sign of x must be different from the sign of y.
(E) The values of x and y must be the same.

188. Which of the following is equivalent to $\dfrac{|x|}{x}$ when $x > 1$?

(A) x
(B) x^{-1}
(C) -1
(D) 0
(E) 1

189. The remainder when an integer m is divided by 2 is 1. What is the remainder when $(m + 1)$ is divided by 2?

(A) 0
(B) 1
(C) 2
(D) 3
(E) 4

190. The median of the following data set is 2. Which of the following is a possible value of x?

x, 2, 1, 6, 7

(A) 2
(B) 3
(C) 5
(D) 6
(E) 8

191. What is the value of $\left(\dfrac{1}{3}\right)^x - \left(\dfrac{1}{2}\right)^y$ when $x = 2$ and $y = -1$?

(A) $-\dfrac{17}{9}$

(B) $-\dfrac{7}{4}$

(C) $-\dfrac{1}{9}$

(D) $\dfrac{1}{8}$

(E) $\dfrac{2}{3}$

192. If the fraction $\dfrac{a}{25}$ is in simplified terms, which of the following CANNOT be a factor of a?

(A) 1
(B) 3
(C) 5
(D) 9
(E) 14

193. If the value of $\dfrac{4^m}{4^n}$ is smaller than 1, which of the following MUST be true?

(A) $m = 1$
(B) $n = 1$
(C) $m = n$
(D) $m < n$
(E) $m > n$

194. If $x > 0$, what is the median of the data set consisting of $-2x$, $-5x$, x, $-8x$, and $4x$?

(A) $-2x$

(B) $-5x$

(C) x

(D) $-8x$

(E) $4x$

195. If 3 and 2 are factors of a, which of the following must be a factor of $14a$?

(A) 4

(B) 5

(C) 8

(D) 11

(E) 19

196. The average of 5 numbers is 20. What is the sum of these same numbers?

(A) 4

(B) 5

(C) 15

(D) 25

(E) 100

MODELING **197.** A professor kept track of the attendance at his Monday-Wednesday-Friday class for one week. The average daily attendance was 32. How many students attended his class on Friday?

Day	Attendance
Monday	32
Wednesday	34
Friday	?

(A) 29

(B) 30

(C) 31

(D) 32

(E) 33

MODELING **198.** To earn a commission for the workweek (Monday through Friday), a salesperson must have average daily sales of $250 or greater for the week. If a salesperson's sales for Monday through Thursday are $98, $255, $175, and $320, what is the LEAST whole number value of sales the salesperson needs to have on Friday to be eligible to earn a commission?

   (A) $250
   (B) $299
   (C) $402
   (D) $1250
   (E) It is not possible for the salesperson to earn a commission this week.

199. How many three-digit numbers have an odd number as a tens digit?

   (A) 25
   (B) 200
   (C) 450
   (D) 500
   (E) 620

MODELING **200.** The average daily rainfall for the past six days is 3.22 inches. How many inches of rain must fall on the seventh day for the average daily rainfall over the past week to be 3.40 inches?

   (A) 2.76
   (B) 3.25
   (C) 3.97
   (D) 4.48
   (E) 4.72

CHAPTER 4

Preparing for Higher Math: Number and Quantity

MODELING

201. The diagram below shows an electric circuit with two batteries and four devices called resistors. I_1, I_2, and I_3 are symbols that represent the values for the electric current in each branch.

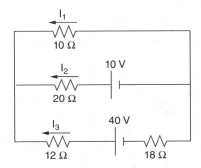

After applying energy and charge conservation, the following three independent equations may be written:

$$I_1 + I_2 + I_3 = 0$$

$$10I_1 + 10 - 20I_2 = 0$$

$$-18I_3 + 40 - 12I_3 + 20I_2 - 10 = 0$$

Which of the following matrix equations best models this problem?

(A) $\begin{bmatrix} 1 & 1 & 1 \\ 10 & -20 & 0 \\ 0 & 20 & -30 \end{bmatrix} \begin{bmatrix} I_1 \\ I_2 \\ I_3 \end{bmatrix} = \begin{bmatrix} 0 \\ -10 \\ -30 \end{bmatrix}$

(B) $\begin{bmatrix} 1 & 1 & 1 \\ 10 & -20 & 0 \\ 0 & 20 & -30 \end{bmatrix} \begin{bmatrix} I_1 \\ I_2 \\ I_3 \end{bmatrix} = \begin{bmatrix} 0 \\ 10 \\ 30 \end{bmatrix}$

(C) $\begin{bmatrix} 1 & 1 & 1 \\ 0 & -20 & 10 \\ -30 & 20 & 0 \end{bmatrix} \begin{bmatrix} I_1 \\ I_2 \\ I_3 \end{bmatrix} = \begin{bmatrix} 0 \\ 10 \\ 30 \end{bmatrix}$

(D) $\begin{bmatrix} 1 & 0 & -30 \\ 1 & -20 & 20 \\ 1 & 10 & 0 \end{bmatrix} \begin{bmatrix} I_1 \\ I_2 \\ I_3 \end{bmatrix} = \begin{bmatrix} 0 \\ 10 \\ 30 \end{bmatrix}$

(E) $\begin{bmatrix} 1 & 0 & -30 \\ 1 & -20 & 20 \\ 1 & 10 & 0 \end{bmatrix} \begin{bmatrix} I_1 \\ I_2 \\ I_3 \end{bmatrix} = \begin{bmatrix} 0 \\ -10 \\ -30 \end{bmatrix}$

202. Given two vectors $\vec{r} = \begin{bmatrix} 2x \\ 3y \end{bmatrix}$ and $\vec{s} = \begin{bmatrix} x-4 \\ 9 \end{bmatrix}$ find the values of x and y if $\vec{r} = \vec{s}$.

(A) $x = 2, y = 3$
(B) $x = 3, y = -4$
(C) $x = -4, y = 3$
(D) $x = -4, y = 9$
(E) $x = 4/3, y = -3$

203. Which of the following is equivalent to $\dfrac{\sqrt{5}}{\sqrt{5}-1}$?

(A) $\dfrac{5+\sqrt{5}}{4}$

(B) $\dfrac{5-\sqrt{5}}{5}$

(C) $1+\sqrt{5}$

(D) $\dfrac{5+\sqrt{5}}{6}$

(E) $1-\sqrt{5}$

204. If a, b, and c are positive integers such that $x = a^{3c}$ and $y = b^{2c}$, then $xy =$

(A) ab^{6c}

(B) ab^{5c}

(C) $(a^3 b^2)^c$

(D) $(ab)^{6c}$

(E) $(ab)^{6c^2}$

205. What is the product of the complex numbers $(4i - 4)$ and $(-2i + 4)$?

(A) $2i$

(B) $24i$

(C) $24i - 24$

(D) $8i^2 - 16$

(E) $24i - 8$

206. What is the difference between $2.\overline{17}$ and 2.17? (Note: A bar over a set of numbers indicates that a digit pattern is repeated.)

(A) 0

(B) 0.17

(C) 0.0017

(D) $0.00\overline{17}$

(E) $0.\overline{0017}$

207. Which of the following is equivalent to $\dfrac{x-3}{x+5}+\dfrac{x}{5}$?

(A) $\dfrac{2x-3}{x+10}$

(B) $\dfrac{x^2-3x}{5x+25}$

(C) $\dfrac{x^2-3x}{5x+5}$

(D) $\dfrac{2x-3}{5(x+5)}$

(E) $\dfrac{x^2+10x-15}{5(x+5)}$

208. If $3^0 = (1-n)^{-3}$, then $n =$

(A) -3
(B) -1
(C) 0
(D) 1
(E) 2

209. $1+\sqrt{-(-5)^2} =$

(A) -4
(B) 6
(C) 26
(D) $1+5i$
(E) $1+25i$

210. If $\left(2^{-\frac{1}{2}}\right)^{4y} = \dfrac{1}{8}$, then $y =$

(A) -4

(B) $-\dfrac{1}{8}$

(C) $\dfrac{7}{8}$

(D) $\dfrac{3}{2}$

(E) $\dfrac{21}{16}$

211. If m is directly proportional to n^2 and $m = 2$ when $n = -1$, then which of the following expressions represents the value of m in terms of x when $n = x + 5$?

(A) $2x + 5$

(B) $2x + 10$

(C) $2x^2 + 10$

(D) $2x^2 + 10x + 25$

(E) $2x^2 + 20x + 50$

212. Which of the following numbers is an imaginary number?

(A) -3^2

(B) $(-5)^2$

(C) $\sqrt{5}$

(D) $\sqrt{-49}$

(E) $-\sqrt{36}$

213. If $m^{-3} = 64$, then $8m =$

(A) -192

(B) -24

(C) $\dfrac{1}{4}$

(D) 2

(E) 32

214. For a real number m, $(2m^3)^4 =$

(A) $2m^7$

(B) $2m^{12}$

(C) $8m^7$

(D) $16m^7$

(E) $16m^{12}$

215. For any real numbers a and b, $(10a^2)(5ab)(2ab^4)$ is equivalent to

(A) $100a^4b^5$

(B) $100a^2b^4$

(C) $17a^4b^5$

(D) $17a^2b^4$

(E) $17a^9b^9$

216. Which of the following is equivalent to i^2, where i is the imaginary number?

(A) -1

(B) 0

(C) 1

(D) $\sqrt{-1}$

(E) $\sqrt{-1^2}$

217. Given $= \begin{bmatrix} 2 & -1 \\ 5 & 3 \end{bmatrix}$ and $N = \begin{bmatrix} 1 & 0 \\ 0 & 1 \end{bmatrix}$, what is the matrix $M - 4N$?

(A) $\begin{bmatrix} 2 & -1 \\ 5 & 3 \end{bmatrix}$

(B) $\begin{bmatrix} 1 & 0 \\ 0 & 1 \end{bmatrix}$

(C) $\begin{bmatrix} -8 & 0 \\ 0 & 12 \end{bmatrix}$

(D) $\begin{bmatrix} -2 & -5 \\ 0 & -1 \end{bmatrix}$

(E) $\begin{bmatrix} -2 & -1 \\ 5 & -1 \end{bmatrix}$

218. Given $6 \begin{bmatrix} x \\ y \end{bmatrix} = 3 \begin{bmatrix} 4 \\ 10 \end{bmatrix}$, find the value of $y - x$.

  (A) 0
  (B) 3
  (C) 5
  (D) 6
  (E) 10

219. Find the magnitude of vector $\vec{r} = \begin{bmatrix} 4 \\ -3 \end{bmatrix}$.

  (A) $\begin{bmatrix} 4 \\ 3 \end{bmatrix}$

  (B) $\begin{bmatrix} -4 \\ 3 \end{bmatrix}$

  (C) 1
  (D) 5
  (E) $\sqrt{7}$

220. If $2^{-m} = \dfrac{1}{8}$, what is the value of m?

  (A) −4
  (B) −3
  (C) 1
  (D) 3
  (E) 4

221. What is the value of $9a - a^2$ when $a = 10$?

  (A) − 90
  (B) − 10
  (C) 70
  (D) 81
  (E) 90

222. For the complex number i such that $i^2 = -1$, which of the following is equivalent to $\dfrac{(i-1)^2}{(i+1)^2}$?

(A) -2
(B) -1
(C) 0
(D) 1
(E) 2

223. If $b \begin{bmatrix} 2 & -1 \\ 5 & 3 \end{bmatrix} = \begin{bmatrix} x & y \\ 5z & 9 \end{bmatrix}$ for some real number b, what is $+y+z$?

(A) 3
(B) 6
(C) 7
(D) 11
(E) 12

224. Which of the following is equivalent to $\left(\dfrac{1}{4m^3} \right)^{-2}$ for any real number m?

(A) $\dfrac{1}{8m}$

(B) $\dfrac{1}{8m^5}$

(C) $\dfrac{1}{16m^6}$

(D) $8m^6$

(E) $16m^6$

225. Let a represent any positive integer. Which of the following is NOT larger than $\left(\dfrac{1}{a}\right)^2$?

(A) a

(B) a^2

(C) $\dfrac{1}{a}$

(D) $\left(\dfrac{2}{a}\right)^2$

(E) $\left(\dfrac{1}{2a}\right)^2$

226. Which of the following is equivalent to $\dfrac{3}{\sqrt{3}} + \dfrac{\sqrt{3}}{\sqrt{6}}$?

(A) $\dfrac{\sqrt{2} + 2\sqrt{3}}{2}$

(B) $9\sqrt{3}$

(C) $\dfrac{5}{2}$

(D) $\dfrac{3 + \sqrt{3}}{\sqrt{3} + \sqrt{6}}$

(E) $3 + \sqrt{6}$

227. Given the function $f(x) = x^3 - 3x$, which of the following is true when $x = 1$?

(A) $f(x) = -3$

(B) $f(x) = -2$

(C) $f(x) = 2$

(D) $f(x) = 3$

(E) $f(x)$ is undefined.

228. Given $A = \begin{bmatrix} 2 & -1 \\ 5 & 3 \end{bmatrix}$ and $B = \begin{bmatrix} 3 & -2 \\ -8 & 5 \end{bmatrix}$, what is $B - A$?

(A) $\begin{bmatrix} -2 & 1 \\ -5 & -3 \end{bmatrix}$

(B) $\begin{bmatrix} 1 & -1 \\ -13 & 2 \end{bmatrix}$

(C) $\begin{bmatrix} 5 & -3 \\ -3 & 8 \end{bmatrix}$

(D) -11

(E) 7

229. For the complex number i such that $i^2 = -1$, what is the value of $\dfrac{i^5}{(i-1)} \times \dfrac{i^8}{(i+1)}$?

(A) $-\dfrac{i}{2}$

(B) $\dfrac{i}{2i-2}$

(C) i

(D) $2i$

(E) $\dfrac{2i}{i-1}$

230. Which of the following is equivalent to $\sqrt[3]{x^{12}}$?

(A) x^{36}

(B) x^{12}

(C) x^{6}

(D) x^{4}

(E) $x^{\frac{4}{3}}$

231. If $0 < x < 16^{\frac{1}{2}}$ and $x = 2^m$ for some positive integer m, what is the value of x?

(A) 1
(B) 2
(C) 4
(D) 6
(E) 8

232. If $2^m = 41$, which of the following inequalities must be true?

(A) $1 < m < 2$
(B) $2 < m < 3$
(C) $3 < m < 4$
(D) $4 < m < 5$
(E) $5 < m < 6$

233. For the complex number i such that $i^2 = -1$, which of the following is equal to $i^4 - i^6$?

(A) -2
(B) -1
(C) 0
(D) 1
(E) 2

234. Given two vectors $\vec{r} = \begin{bmatrix} 2 \\ 1 \end{bmatrix}$ and $\vec{s} = \begin{bmatrix} -2 \\ 0 \end{bmatrix}$, find the magnitude of $5\vec{r} - \vec{s}$.

(A) $\begin{bmatrix} 12 \\ 5 \end{bmatrix}$

(B) 6
(C) 12
(D) 13

(E) $\begin{bmatrix} 12 \\ 6 \end{bmatrix}$

235. If $\dfrac{3^p}{3^q} = 81$, which of the following statements must be true?

(A) The sum of p and q must be 81.
(B) The difference of p and q must be 4.
(C) Both p and q must be integers.
(D) Both p and q must be positive.
(E) Either p or q must be positive.

236. For which of the following values of x is the value of $g(x) = -x^2 + 10$ negative?

(A) -4
(B) -3
(C) -2
(D) -1
(E) 3

237. For what values of a is the inequality $a^2 \leq a$ always true?

(A) $a < 0$
(B) $a > 0$
(C) $0 \leq a \leq 1$
(D) $a > 1$ and $a < -1$
(E) The inequality is not true for any value of a.

238. If $f(x) = 2x(1-x)^2$, then $f(1) =$

(A) 0
(B) 2
(C) 4
(D) 6
(E) 8

239. If $3^m = 1$, which of the following is a possible value of m?

(A) -1
(B) 0
(C) 1
(D) 2
(E) 3

240. Suppose y^2 is inversely proportional to x and $y^2 = 16$ when $x = 4$. Which of the following is the value of y^2 when $x = 2$?

(A) 4
(B) $\sqrt{21}$
(C) $4\sqrt{2}$
(D) 8
(E) 32

241. Simplify the following expression: $\dfrac{(2)^{\frac{20}{3}}}{(4)^{\frac{5}{2}}}$

   (A) $\sqrt[3]{2^8}$

   (B) $\sqrt[5]{2^3}$

   (C) $\sqrt[3]{2^5}$

   (D) $\sqrt[5]{2}$

   (E) $\sqrt[3]{2}$

242. If y is inversely proportional to the square root of x and if y has a value of 18 when x is 4, what is the value of y when x is 12?

   (A) $\dfrac{\sqrt{3}}{9}$

   (B) $\dfrac{\sqrt{6}}{9}$

   (C) $\dfrac{\sqrt{3}}{3}$

   (D) $3\sqrt{2}$

   (E) $6\sqrt{3}$

243. How many imaginary roots does the function $g(x) = x^2 + 1$ have?

   (A) 0

   (B) 1

   (C) 2

   (D) 3

   (E) 4

244. If $x = 4$ and $y = -1$, then $xy^4 + x^3y =$

   (A) -8

   (B) -16

   (C) -18

   (D) -60

   (E) -68

245. What is the value of $(-x)^2 - (-x)$ when $x = -2$?

(A) −4

(B) −2

(C) 0

(D) 2

(E) 4

246. Which of the following expressions is equivalent to $(2m - 6)^2$ for all values of m?

(A) $4m^2 - 12$

(B) $4m^2 - 24$

(C) $4m^2 - 36$

(D) $4m^2 - 24x + 36$

(E) $4m^2 - 12x + 36$

247. What is the value of $f(x) = \dfrac{x^3}{4}$ when $x = \dfrac{1}{2}$?

(A) $\dfrac{1}{32}$

(B) $\dfrac{1}{16}$

(C) $\dfrac{1}{12}$

(D) $\dfrac{1}{8}$

(E) $\dfrac{1}{2}$

248. Evaluate the following matrix: $-2\begin{bmatrix} 5 & -2 & 3 \\ 0 & 10 & -5 \end{bmatrix}$.

(A) $\begin{bmatrix} -10 & 4 & -6 \\ 0 & -20 & 10 \end{bmatrix}$

(B) -22

(C) $\begin{bmatrix} 5 & 0 \\ -2 & 10 \\ 3 & -5 \end{bmatrix}$

(D) -19

(E) $\begin{bmatrix} -\dfrac{5}{2} & 1 & -\dfrac{3}{2} \\ 0 & -5 & \dfrac{5}{2} \end{bmatrix}$

249. Which of the following expressions is equivalent to $\left(\dfrac{1}{2}x^2 y\right)^5$ for all x and y?

(A) $\dfrac{1}{10}x^{10}y^5$

(B) $\dfrac{1}{10}x^7 y^5$

(C) $\dfrac{1}{32}x^{10}y^5$

(D) $\dfrac{1}{32}x^7 y^5$

(E) $\dfrac{5}{32}x^{10}y^5$

250. For the complex number i such that $i^2 = -1$, which of the following is equal to $\dfrac{i^4 - 5}{i^2}$?

(A) -7
(B) -6
(C) -5
(D) 4
(E) 24

CHAPTER 5

Preparing for Higher Math: Algebra

Use the following information to answer questions 251–252.

The owner of Pizza Mania wants to analyze the profit from her business. It costs her $200 each day for labor and an additional $160 per day for rent and utilities. For her average pizza, the ingredients cost $2 and the selling price is $14.

251. Write an algebraic function that models the owners daily cost per pizza based on the number (n) of pizzas sold.

(A) $360 + 2n$

(B) $2n$

(C) $\dfrac{360 + 2n}{n}$

(D) $\dfrac{360 + 10n}{n}$

(E) $10n - 360$

252. How many pizzas does the owner have to sell each day before she starts to earn a profit?

(A) 20

(B) 23

(C) 25

(D) 30

(E) 32

253. For what values of x is $x^2 - 3x - 10 = 0$?

    (A) $x = 3$
    (B) $x = 10$
    (C) $x = 5$
    (D) $x = 3$ and $x = 10$
    (E) $x = 5$ and $x = -2$

254. If $\dfrac{m}{4} = \dfrac{m-1}{3}$, then $m =$

    (A) -5
    (B) -1
    (C) 3
    (D) 4
    (E) 9

255. If $x - y = -5$ and $x + y = 1$, then $xy =$

    (A) -6
    (B) -2
    (C) 1
    (D) 3
    (E) 12

256. In the matrix product shown, what is the value of x?

$$\begin{bmatrix} -1 & 2 \\ 4 & 8 \end{bmatrix} \begin{bmatrix} 6 & 3 \\ 7 & -6 \end{bmatrix} = \begin{bmatrix} x & y \\ z & w \end{bmatrix}$$

    (A) -6
    (B) 5
    (C) 8
    (D) 14
    (E) 20

257. Which of the following is a root of $-5x + x^2$?

    (A) -5
    (B) -3
    (C) 1
    (D) 3
    (E) 5

258. For what values of m is $m^2 - 8m + 15 < 0$?

    (A) $m < 3$

    (B) $m > 3$

    (C) $m < 5$

    (D) $m > 5$

    (E) $3 < m < 5$

259. The sum of two consecutive odd integers is 256. What is the value of the larger integer?

    (A)   103

    (B)   127

    (C)   129

    (D)   153

    (E)   155

260. If $\dfrac{2p+q}{p} > 5$ and $p > 2$, which of the following inequalities MUST be true?

    (A) $q > 0$

    (B) $q > 2$

    (C) $q > 6$

    (D) $q > 10$

    (E) $q > 12$

261. When $x \neq 0$, $\dfrac{x^2 - 4x^2 + x^2}{x} =$

    (A) $-2x^6$

    (B) $-2x^5$

    (C) $-2x^4$

    (D) $-2x^2$

    (E) $-2x$

262. For all values of a and b, which of the following expressions is equivalent to $(a - 6)(b + 4)$?

    (A) $ab - 24$

    (B) $ab - 2$

    (C) $a^2b - 2ab - 24$

    (D) $a^2b - 2ab - 2$

    (E) $ab + 4a - 6b - 24$

263. For what values of m and n would the following system of equations have infinite solutions?

$-3x + y = 2$

$mx + ny = -6$

(A) $m = -3, n = -4$

(B) $m = -3, n = 1$

(C) $m = 9, n = 1$

(D) $m = 9, n = -3$

(E) $m = 3, n = -1$

264. What is the smallest integer for which the inequality $\dfrac{x}{4} - \dfrac{1}{4} \geq 1$ is true?

(A) 4

(B) 5

(C) 6

(D) 7

(E) 8

265. Which of the following equations will always have the same solution or solutions as the equation $4xy - 1 = \dfrac{x}{2} + \dfrac{y}{3}$?

(A) $4xy + 4 = 3x + 2y$

(B) $8xy - 1 = 3x + 2y$

(C) $12xy - 3 = 3x + 2y$

(D) $20xy - 5 = 3x + 2y$

(E) $24xy - 6 = 3x + 2y$

266. Which of the following inequalities represents the set of all values of x that satisfy the inequality $-3x + 4 > 6$?

(A) $x < -\dfrac{2}{3}$

(B) $x > -\dfrac{2}{3}$

(C) $x < -\dfrac{10}{3}$

(D) $x > -\dfrac{10}{3}$

(E) $-\dfrac{10}{3} < x < -\dfrac{2}{3}$

267. What value of a is a solution to the inequality $a - x \geq c$ but is not a solution to the inequality $a - x > c$?

(A) $a = -c$

(B) $a = c$

(C) $a = cx$

(D) $a = c + x$

(E) $a = c - x$

268. If $3^{xy} = \dfrac{1}{9}$, $2x + y = 0$, and x is positive, then $x + y =$

(A) -3

(B) -1

(C) 2

(D) 6

(E) 9

269. If $k = -1$, then $\left(\dfrac{x + y}{k} \right)^2 =$

(A) $-(x^2 + y^2)$

(B) $x^2 + y^2$

(C) $x^2 + 2xy + y^2$

(D) $-(x^2 + 2xy + y^2)$

(E) $x^2 - 2xy - y^2$

270. If $\log_2 x = 3$, what is the value of x?

(A) 1

(B) 2

(C) 6

(D) 8

(E) 9

271. The expression $(x - a)(x + a) =$

(A) $x^2 - 2a$

(B) $x^2 - a^2$

(C) $x^2 - 2a - a^2$

(D) $x^2 - 2a + a^2$

(E) $x^2 + 2a - a^2$

272. If $3x^2 - \dfrac{1}{2}x = 0$ and $x > 0$, what is the value of x?

(A) $\dfrac{1}{6}$

(B) $\dfrac{1}{2}$

(C) $\dfrac{3}{2}$

(D) 3

(E) 6

273. For what values of b and c would the following system of equations have no solutions?

$$2x + 8y = 2$$
$$x + by = c$$

(A) $b = 4, c = 1$
(B) $b = 4, c = 3$
(C) $b = 8, c = 4$
(D) $b = 8, c = -2$
(E) $b = 8, c = 2$

274. If $3m - 4 = 6n - 8$, which of the following expressions is equivalent to $3m - 8$?

(A) $6n$
(B) $6n - 12$
(C) $6n - 8$
(D) $6n - 4$
(E) $6n + 4$

275. For all nonzero values of x and y, $a = \dfrac{x}{y}$. If $b = 2a - a^2$, which of the following expressions defines b in terms of x and y?

(A) $\dfrac{x - x^2}{y}$

(B) $\dfrac{2x - x^2}{y}$

(C) $\dfrac{2x - x^2}{2y^2}$

(D) $\dfrac{2xy - x^2}{y^2}$

(E) $\dfrac{xy - x^2}{y^2}$

276. If $A = \begin{bmatrix} -1 & 2 \\ 4 & 9 \end{bmatrix}$ and $B = \begin{bmatrix} 0 & -8 \\ 1 & 1 \end{bmatrix}$ such that $A - B = \begin{bmatrix} x & y \\ z & w \end{bmatrix}$, what is the value of z?

(A) −1
(B) 0
(C) 3
(D) 4
(E) 5

277. The expression $\dfrac{6x - 4}{2}$ is equivalent to which of the following?

(A) $3x - 2$
(B) $3x - 4$
(C) $6x - 2$
(D) $6x - 4$
(E) $12x - 8$

278. If $4(x - 1) = 8(x - 2)$, then $x =$

(A) −2
(B) −1
(C) 1
(D) 3
(E) 4

279. How many positive integers satisfy the inequality $-5 \geq -7x$?

   (A) None
   (B) One
   (C) Two
   (D) Three
   (E) Infinitely many

280. The sum of the terms $3x$, $4x - 1$, and $-2x$ is 9. What is the value of x?

   (A) 1
   (B) 2
   (C) 5
   (D) 10
   (E) Cannot be determined from the given information

281. Which of the following values of a makes the equation $\dfrac{1}{2a} + \dfrac{1}{a} = 14$ true?

   (A) $\dfrac{3}{28}$

   (B) $\dfrac{1}{14}$

   (C) $\dfrac{14}{3}$

   (D) 14
   (E) 16

MODELING **282.** Last week, a student began collecting rare coins. Since then, he has doubled his collection by obtaining 36 more coins than he started with. How many coins are currently in his collection?

   (A) 18
   (B) 36
   (C) 72
   (D) 84
   (E) 116

283. Each of the following integers satisfies the inequality $-\dfrac{1}{2} \leq 5x \leq \dfrac{33}{2}$ EXCEPT

   (A) 0
   (B) 1
   (C) 2
   (D) 3
   (E) 4

284. If the smallest of three consecutive integers is x, which of the following expressions represents their sum?

(A) $3x$
(B) $x + 3$
(C) $3x + 1$
(D) $3x + 3$
(E) $3x + 6$

285. Which of the following expressions is equivalent to $5x - \dfrac{15}{2}$?

(A) $-10x$
(B) $-5x$

(C) $5\left(x - \dfrac{1}{2}\right)$

(D) $5\left(x - \dfrac{3}{2}\right)$

(E) $5\left(x - \dfrac{15}{2}\right)$

286. If $a - b = 7$ and $2a + b = -1$, then $b =$

(A) -5
(B) -3
(C) 2
(D) 4
(E) 8

MODELING **287.** A company that sells two types of paper keeps twice as much of Type 1 in stock as it keeps of Type 2. Currently, the company has a total of 21,000 pounds of paper in stock. How many pounds of Type 2 paper does the company currently have in stock?

(A) 7000
(B) 10,500
(C) 14,000
(D) 18,500
(E) 42,000

288. What is the value of a when $6a - 1 = 2(a + 1)$?

    (A) $\dfrac{3}{8}$

    (B) $\dfrac{3}{4}$

    (C) $\dfrac{1}{2}$

    (D) 0

    (E) $\dfrac{5}{2}$

289. For what positive value of x is $3x^2 - 19x = 14$?

    (A) 2

    (B) 3

    (C) 7

    (D) 14

    (E) 19

290. If $mn = 4$, then $6(m^2 n^2 - 1) =$

    (A) 15

    (B) 23

    (C) 42

    (D) 90

    (E) 95

291. Which of the following is equivalent to the expression $3a^2 - 2b^2 + b$?

    (A) $2a^2 b^2 b$

    (B) $a^2 b^2 + b$

    (C) $3a^2 - b(2b + 1)$

    (D) $3a^2 - b(2b - 1)$

    (E) $3a^2 - 2b(b + 1)$

292. If $x = \dfrac{1}{2}$, then $(2y-1)^{-x} =$

(A) $y + \dfrac{1}{2}$

(B) $2y + \dfrac{1}{2}$

(C) $\sqrt{y + \dfrac{1}{2}}$

(D) $\sqrt{-2y+1}$

(E) $\dfrac{1}{\sqrt{2y-1}}$

293. Which of the following inequalities has the same solution set as $x - 8 \geq 5x + 1$?

(A) $-x + 8 \leq 5x + 1$
(B) $-x + 8 \leq -5x - 1$
(C) $x - 8 \leq -5x + 1$
(D) $x - 8 \leq -5x - 1$
(E) $-x - 8 \leq -5x - 1$

294. Which operation in place of the Δ in the following equation would make the equation true for all nonzero values of x?

$$x^2 \Delta\, 2x = \dfrac{x}{2}$$

(A) $\times$
(B) $+$
(C) $-$
(D) $\div$
(E) Cannot be determined from the given information

295. The product of two numbers is 20, while their sum is 12. What is the difference of the two numbers?

(A) 8
(B) 17
(C) 33
(D) 188
(E) 212

296. For what value(s) of y is $x - y > x + y$ true for any possible value of x?

(A) $y = 0$
(B) $y = 1$
(C) $y < 0$
(D) $y > 0$
(E) $y > 1$

297. If $\log_3(x - 1) = 2$, what is the value of x?

(A) 3
(B) 4
(C) 7
(D) 9
(E) 10

298. How many roots larger than 5 does $x^2 - 3x + 2$ have?

(A) None
(B) One
(C) Two
(D) Three
(E) Cannot be determined from the given information

299. Which of the following represents the solution set to the inequality $-\dfrac{1}{2}x + 5 \geq 9$?

(A) $x \leq -8$
(B) $x \leq -4$
(C) $x \leq 0$
(D) $x \leq 4$
(E) $x \leq 8$

300. What is the value of x if the following equations are true?

$$2x - y = -8$$
$$3x + 2y = 2$$

(A) -4
(B) -2
(C) 4
(D) 10
(E) 12

301. For what value of x is $\log_x 16 = 4$?

(A) 1
(B) 2
(C) 4
(D) 8
(E) 16

302. For positive values of m, $\dfrac{m}{\sqrt{m}}$ is equivalent to which of the following expressions?

(A) 1
(B) m
(C) m^2
(D) $\sqrt{m}$
(E) $m\sqrt{m}$

303. The product of a and $(a - 1)$ is 6. Which of the following is a possible value of a?

(A) 2
(B) $\dfrac{5}{2}$
(C) 3
(D) $\dfrac{7}{2}$
(E) 6

304. A number x can be written in the form $k^2 - 2$ for some integer value of k. Which of the following expressions represents x^2 in terms of k?

(A) $k^4 - 4$
(B) $2k^2 - 4$
(C) $k^4 - k^2 + 4$
(D) $k^4 - 4k^2 + 2$
(E) $k^4 - 4k^2 + 4$

305. $(3x^2 - 5x + 1) - (3x^2 - 2x + 6) =$

(A) $-3x - 5$

(B) $-3x + 7$

(C) $-7x - 7$

(D) $-7x - 5$

(E) $-7x + 7$

306. What is the greatest common factor of $2a^4$ and a^3?

(A) a

(B) a^3

(C) $2a$

(D) $2a^4$

(E) $2a^7$

307. If $\sqrt{y} + 8 = 3\sqrt{y}$, then $y =$

(A) 2

(B) 4

(C) 16

(D) 25

(E) 64

308. Which of the following expressions in place of the square would make the expression $10n^3 - 5n^2 = \square(2n^2 - n)$ true for any value of n?

(A) 5

(B) n

(C) $5n$

(D) $5n^2$

(E) n^3

309. Which of the following values of x makes the equation $x - 5 = 9 - x$ true?

(A) 2

(B) 4

(C) 7

(D) 14

(E) The equation is not true for any value of x.

310. If $p - 5 > -2$, then which of the following inequalities must be true?

(A) $p + 5 > -12$

(B) $p + 5 > -3$

(C) $p + 5 > 0$

(D) $p + 5 > 2$

(E) $p + 5 > 8$

311. If $-k^2 = k$, which of the following is a possible value of k?

(A) -4

(B) -3

(C) -2

(D) -1

(E) 1

312. Which of the following is equivalent to the expression $\dfrac{1 - x^2}{x}$ for all nonzero values of x?

(A) $\dfrac{1}{x}$

(B) $\dfrac{1}{x} - 1$

(C) $\dfrac{1}{x} - x$

(D) $\dfrac{1}{x} - x^2$

(E) $\dfrac{1}{x} - x^3$

MODELING **313.** A prize of $\$m$ is to be divided evenly among 6 people. In terms of m, which of the following expressions represents the total amount of prize money 2 of the 6 people will receive?

(A) $\dfrac{m}{6}$

(B) $\dfrac{m}{5}$

(C) $\dfrac{m}{4}$

(D) $\dfrac{m}{3}$

(E) $\dfrac{m}{2}$

314. If $2x + y^2 = 7$ and $y^2 = 3x$, then $10x =$

(A) 8
(B) 10
(C) 12
(D) 14
(E) 19

315. For $x \neq 0$, $\dfrac{2x}{9} \times \dfrac{3}{x} =$

(A) $\dfrac{1}{3}$

(B) $\dfrac{1}{2}$

(C) $\dfrac{2}{3}$

(D) $\dfrac{2x^2}{27}$

(E) $\dfrac{x^2}{4}$

316. If $x > 0$, which of the following expressions will have the smallest value?

$$-2x, \frac{x}{2}, x^2, \frac{x}{4}, x^3$$

(A) $-2x$

(B) $\dfrac{x}{2}$

(C) x^2

(D) $\dfrac{x}{4}$

(E) x^3

317. Given the equation $2(x+1) = -(y+2)$, when $y = 0$, which of the following is the value of x?

(A) -4

(B) -2

(C) 0

(D) 3

(E) 5

318. What is the least common denominator of $\dfrac{3}{8a}$ and $\dfrac{1}{6a}$?

(A) $6a$

(B) $8a$

(C) $14a$

(D) $24a$

(E) $48a$

319. The sum of a number n and 4 is 10. What is the value of the sum of n and -1?

(A) 2

(B) 3

(C) 5

(D) 9

(E) 11

320. Which of the following is a possible value of x if $4x > 3$ and $-x > 3$?

(A) -5

(B) -3

(C) 1

(D) 8

(E) There are no values of x that satisfy both inequalities.

CHAPTER 6

Preparing for Higher Math: Functions

Use the following information to answer questions 321–322.

Mario enters a highway at mile marker 299 and travels south from Ft. Wayne toward Indianapolis, driving at an average speed of 50 miles per hour. He wants to rendezvous with Kiyomi, who is entering the same highway at mile marker 203 and driving north toward Ft. Wayne at an average speed of 70 miles per hour.

MODELING

321. Which of the following functions best models Mario's mile marker position (M) as a function of the hours of elapsed time (t)?

(A) $M = -50t + 299$
(B) $M = 50t + 299$
(C) $M = 50t - 299$
(D) $M = -70t + 299$
(E) $M = 70t + 203$

MODELING

322. How many minutes will it take for Mario and Kiyomi to reach the same mile marker?

(A) 48 minutes
(B) 60 minutes
(C) 130 minutes
(D) 144 minutes
(E) 288 minutes

323. Which of the following is a factor of $x^2 - x - 12$?

(A) x
(B) $x - 1$
(C) $x - 3$
(D) $x - 4$
(E) $x - 12$

324. Let $a \, \Xi \, b = b^2 - a^2 + 1$ for any real numbers a and b. What is the value of $(-2) \, \Xi \, (-3)$?

(A) -12
(B) -4
(C) 3
(D) 6
(E) 14

325. The functions f and g are defined as $g(x) = mx + b$ for nonzero values of m and b, and $f(x) = ax^2 + bx + c$ for nonzero values of a, b, and c. In the standard (x, y) coordinate plane, what is the maximum number of times the graphs of $f(x)$ and $g(x)$ can cross each other?

(A) 1
(B) 2
(C) 3
(D) 4
(E) 5

326. In the standard (x, y) coordinate plane, a polynomial function $f(x)$ crosses the x-axis at the points $(-3, 0)$, $(-2, 0)$, $(4, 0)$, $(5, 0)$, and $(7, 0)$ only. Each of the following is a factor of $f(x)$ EXCEPT

(A) $x - 3$
(B) $x - 4$
(C) $x - 7$
(D) $x - 5$
(E) $x + 2$

327. If the graph of $f(x) = x^2 - 1$ is shifted to the left by 3 units, which of the following expressions will represent the resulting graph?

(A) $x^2 - 4$
(B) $(x - 3)^2 - 1$
(C) $x^2 + 2$
(D) $(x + 3)^2 - 1$
(E) $x^2 - 3$

328. In the standard (x, y) coordinate plane, the graph of the function $f(x) = 3x - 5$ crosses through the point $(q, 4)$. What is the value of q?

(A) 2
(B) 3
(C) 5
(D) 7
(E) 9

MODELING **329.** The value of an investment grows based on the function $V(t) = 1000(1 + 0.06)^t$, where V is the value in dollars and t is the time in years. To the nearest cent, what is the value of the investment after 8 years?

(A) $1068.48
(B) $1410.09
(C) $1593.85
(D) $1604.66
(E) $1790.85

330. If $f(x)$ is graphed in the following figure, then which of the following is a possible formula for $f(x)$?

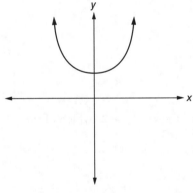

(A) x^2
(B) $(x - 4)^2$
(C) $(x + 3)^2$
(D) $x^2 - 2$
(E) $x^2 + 4$

331. In the standard (x, y) coordinate plane, which of the following statements best describes the graph of $-f(x)$ in terms of the graph of $f(x)$ for any function $f(x)$?

(A) It is the graph of $f(x)$ shifted downward by one unit.
(B) It is the graph of $f(x)$ shifted upward by one unit.
(C) It is the graph of $f(x)$ shifted to the left by one unit.
(D) It is the graph of $f(x)$ shifted to the right by one unit.
(E) None of these statements is correct.

332. If $f(x) = x^2 + x - 1$, which of the following expressions is equivalent to $f(a-1)$?

(A) $a^2 - a$
(B) $a^2 - 3a$
(C) $a^2 + a - 2$
(D) $a^2 - a - 1$
(E) $a^2 - 3a - 2$

333. Define $a \: \nabla \: b = 2a - 3b$ for all integers a and b. What is the value of $-2 \: \nabla \: 1$?

(A) -7
(B) -4
(C) -1
(D) 1
(E) 8

334. Given the functions $f(x) = x + 6$ and $g(x) = x^2 - 2$, which of the following is the value of $(f \circ g)(3)$?

(A) 7
(B) 9
(C) 10
(D) 13
(E) 79

335. In the standard (x, y) coordinate plane, the graphs of $f(x) = 8$ and $g(x) = 64x^3$ intersect at the point (a, b) in the first quadrant. What is the value of a?

(A) $\dfrac{1}{8}$

(B) $\dfrac{1}{2}$

(C) 2

(D) 4

(E) 8

336. What is the value of $g(x) = x^4 + x^2$ if $x = \sqrt{3}$?

(A) 9

(B) $6\sqrt{3}$

(C) 12

(D) $15\sqrt{3}$

(E) 15

337. What is the largest value of x that makes the equation $x^2 + 2x - 35 = 0$ true?

(A) 5

(B) 7

(C) 12

(D) 33

(E) 35

338. The graph of a polynomial function crosses the x-axis at the points A, B, and C as indicated in the following figure.

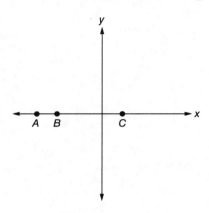

If the graph does not cross the x-axis at any other point, which of the following could be the formula for the function?

(A) $f(x) = (x + 3)(x + 4)(x - 1)$
(B) $f(x) = (x + 3)(x - 4)(x - 1)$
(C) $f(x) = (x - 3)(x - 4)(x - 1)$
(D) $f(x) = (x + 3)(x + 4)(x + 1)$
(E) Cannot be determined from the given information

339. If $2x^2 - 6x = -4$ and $x < 0$, then $x =$

(A) -6
(B) -4
(C) -2
(D) -1
(E) There is no such value of x.

340. Which of the following is a factor of $x^4 - 16$?

(A) $x - 16$
(B) $x - 8$
(C) $x - 4$
(D) $x - 2$
(E) x

341. The following table represents values of a function $f(x)$ for the given values of x. Which of the following must be a solution to the equation $f(x) = 0$?

x	-6	-3	0
$f(x)$	0	1	4

(A) -6
(B) -4
(C) -3
(D) 1
(E) 4

342. Which of the following functions has the same roots as $f(x) = 3x^2 - 3x - 27$?

(A) $f_1(x) = x^2 - 3x - 27$

(B) $f_2(x) = 3x^2 - x - 27$

(C) $f_3(x) = 3x^2 - 3x - 3$

(D) $f_4(x) = x^2 - x - 3$

(E) $f_5(x) = x^2 - x - 9$

MODELING **343.** If the following steps evaluate a function g at the value x, then $g(x) =$

Step 1: Add 3 to x.
Step 2: Square the result of step 1.
Step 3: Multiply the result of step 2 by 5.

(A) $(5x + 3)^2$

(B) $5(x + 3)^2$

(C) $5(x^2 + 3)$

(D) $(5x)^2 + 3$

(E) $5x^2 + 3$

344. If $f(r, s) = rs - r$, then $f(2, -3) =$

(A) -8
(B) -4
(C) 1
(D) 6
(E) 7

345. If $f(x) = x^3$, which of the following tables would correctly represent the values of $-f(x)$ when x is -2, -1, 0, 1, and 2?

(A)

x	-2	-1	0	1	2
$-f(x)$	-8	-1	0	1	8

(B)

x	-2	-1	0	1	2
$-f(x)$	-8	-1	0	-1	-8

(C)

x	-2	-1	0	1	2
$-f(x)$	8	1	0	-1	-8

(D)

x	-2	-1	0	1	2
$-f(x)$	8	-1	0	-1	8

(E)

x	-2	-1	0	1	2
$-f(x)$	8	1	0	1	8

346. If the point (a, b) lies on the graph of a function $f(x)$ in the standard (x, y) coordinate plane, then which of the following points lies along the graph of $f(x - 2)$?

(A) $(-2a, b)$
(B) $(a, -2b)$
(C) $(a - 2, b)$
(D) $(a, b - 2)$
(E) $(a + 2, b)$

347. Let $x \Delta y = \dfrac{x+1}{y}$ for positive integers x and y. What is the value of $7\Delta(-2)$?

(A) -4
(B) -1
(C) 3
(D) 8
(E) 14

348. If, for a nonzero value of k, $f(x) = \dfrac{x-3}{k}$ and $f(2) = 2$, then $k =$

(A) -3

(B) -2

(C) $-\dfrac{1}{2}$

(D) $-\dfrac{1}{6}$

(E) 6

349. If $f(x) = x^2$ and $g(x) = 72 - x$, what is the smallest value of x for which $f(x) = g(x)$?

(A) -9

(B) -8

(C) 0

(D) 8

(E) 9

350. If a, b, and c are nonzero real numbers, what is the least number of times a function $f(x) = ax^2 + bx + c$ may cross the x-axis?

(A) 0

(B) 1

(C) 2

(D) 3

(E) Cannot be determined without the values of a, b, and c

351. Given the graph of $g(x)$ shown in the figure, which of the following graphs is of the function $-g(x)$?

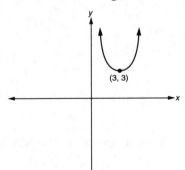

(A)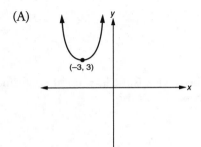

(B)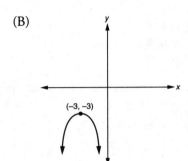

(C)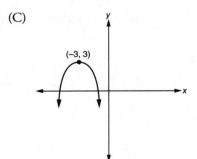

(D)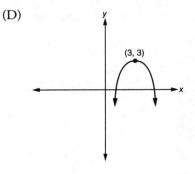

(E)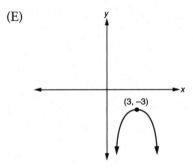

352. If $x > 0$ and $2x^2 - 5x + 3 = x^2 - 5x + 2$, then $x =$

    (A) 1

    (B) 2

    (C) 3

    (D) 5

    (E) There are no such real values of x.

353. The following figure represents the graph of a function $f(x)$ whose y-intercept is located at $(0, 2)$ and whose x-intercept is located at $(-4, 0)$. For what values of x must $f(x) > 0$?

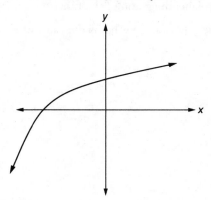

    (A) $x < -4$

    (B) $-4 < x < 2$

    (C) $x < 2$

    (D) $x > -4$

    (E) $x > 2$

354. If $f(x) = \dfrac{x-4}{x+1}$ for all nonzero values of x, then $f(5) =$

    (A) -4

    (B) $\dfrac{1}{6}$

    (C) 1

    (D) $\dfrac{3}{2}$

    (E) 5

MODELING **355.** The number of patients seen by a doctor over a day is represented by the function $P(t) = 8t - 5$, where P is the total number of patients seen after t hours. Based on this function, how many patients are seen between hours 5 and 6?

(A) 3
(B) 5
(C) 8
(D) 10
(E) 13

356. In the standard (x, y) coordinate plane, the graph of the function $g(x) = \dfrac{3x + 10}{8}$ passes through the point $(4, c)$. What is the value of c?

(A) $\dfrac{4}{3}$

(B) $\dfrac{3}{2}$

(C) $\dfrac{17}{8}$

(D) $\dfrac{11}{4}$

(E) $\dfrac{22}{3}$

357. If one factor of a polynomial function is $x - k$, then which of the following must be a zero of the function?

(A) $-k$

(B) $-\dfrac{k}{2}$

(C) 0

(D) $\dfrac{k}{2}$

(E) k

358. If $f(x) = \dfrac{1}{2}x^2$ and $g(x) = 2x$, then for what value or values of x is $f(g(x)) = 8$?

(A) -2 only

(B) -2 and 2 only

(C) 2 only

(D) $2\sqrt{2}$ only

(E) $-2\sqrt{2}$ and $2\sqrt{2}$ only

359. The graph of a function $g(x)$ is found by shifting the graph of the function $f(x)$ up by 6 units and to the left by 1 unit. If $f(x) = (x-5)^3$, then $g(x) =$

(A) x^3

(B) $(x-2)^3$

(C) $(x+1)^3 - 1$

(D) $(x-6)^3 + 6$

(E) $(x-4)^3 + 6$

360. Let the function $f(x)$ be defined as $f(x) = -x^2 + c$ for a positive value of c. If the function crosses the x-axis at the points -3 and 3, then which of the following must be true about $f(x)$ if $x < -3$?

  I. $f(x)$ has the same possible values if $x > 3$.

  II. $f(x) < 0$

  III. $f(x) > c$

(A) I only

(B) II only

(C) III only

(D) I and II only

(E) I and III only

361. If $g(a,b) = 4ab - b + a$, then for what values of b is $g(1,b) > 0$?

(A) $b < -\dfrac{1}{3}$

(B) $b > -\dfrac{1}{5}$

(C) $b > -\dfrac{1}{3}$

(D) $b > -1$

(E) $b < 4$

362. If $f(x) = x + 10$ and $g(x) = -5x - 8$, then $(f \circ g)(7) =$

(A) −93
(B) −85
(C) −43
(D) −33
(E) −29

363. Given the following graphs of $f(x)$ and $g(x)$ in the standard (x, y) coordinate plane, for what values of x is $g(x) > f(x)$?

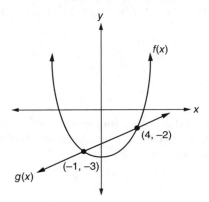

(A) $x < -1$ and $x > 4$
(B) $-1 < x < 4$
(C) $x < -3$
(D) $x < 4$
(E) $x > -2$

364. For fixed real values of a, b, and c, a solution to the equation $ax^2 + bx + c = 0$ is $-\dfrac{5}{2}$. For the same values of a, b, and c, which of the following is a factor of the expression $ax^2 + bx + c$?

(A) $2x - 5$
(B) $2x + 5$
(C) $-5x - 2$
(D) $-5x + 2$
(E) $5x - 2$

365. For all values of $x \neq 4$, the function $f(x) = \dfrac{x^2 - 3x - 4}{x - 4}$ has the same value as

(A) $-7x$

(B) $-3x$

(C) $-\dfrac{3}{4}x + 1$

(D) $-3x + 1$

(E) $x + 1$

366. In the (x, y) coordinate plane, which of the following functions would have a graph that crosses or touches the x-axis at only one point?

(A) $x^2 + 5$

(B) $x^2 - 6$

(C) $x^2 - 8x + 16$

(D) $x^2 + 2x + 18$

(E) $-x^2 + 4x - 10$

367. Which of the following is equivalent to $g(a^2 - 10)$ when $g(x) = x^2 + x - 5$?

(A) $a^4 + 20a^2 + 85$

(B) $a^4 + a^2 - 115$

(C) $a^4 + a^2 + 85$

(D) $a^4 - 19a^2 - 115$

(E) $a^4 - 19a^2 + 85$

368. Which of the following points is on the graph of the function $f(x) = (x - 5)$ $(x + 3)(x - 1)(x + 10)$?

(A) $(0, 0)$

(B) $(5, 0)$

(C) $(0, -3)$

(D) $(-1, 0)$

(E) $(0, 10)$

369. Let a, b, and c represent any three real numbers where $a < 0$. If a quadratic function $f(x) = ax^2 + bx + c$ has x-intercepts of $(3, 0)$ and $(9, 0)$, then which of the following must be true about $f(4)$?

(A) The value of $f(4)$ is negative.
(B) The value of $f(4)$ is positive.
(C) The value of $f(4)$ is zero.
(D) The value of $f(4)$ is between -5 and 5.
(E) The value of $f(4)$ is undefinable.

370. If one of the solutions to the equation $(x - 5)(x + 2)(ax - b) = 0$ is -7, then which of the following pairs of values for a and b is possible?

(A) $a = -7$, $b = 1$
(B) $a = 1$, $b = -7$
(C) $a = 7$, $b = 1$
(D) $a = 1$, $b = 7$
(E) $a = -1$, $b = -7$

371. The complete graph of a function $f(x)$ is shown in the following figure. How many real solutions does the equation $f(x) = 0$ have?

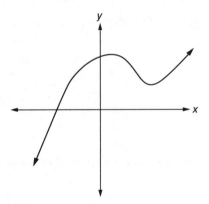

(A) 0
(B) 1
(C) 2
(D) 3
(E) 4

372. Given the following table of values for a function $f(x)$, which of the following is the solution to the equation $\dfrac{f(2)}{4} = 12x$?

x	1	2	3
$f(x)$	2	8	10

(A) $\dfrac{1}{48}$

(B) $\dfrac{1}{12}$

(C) $\dfrac{1}{6}$

(D) $\dfrac{1}{4}$

(E) $\dfrac{1}{3}$

373. In the (x, y) coordinate plane, the graphs of $f(x) = 2x^2 + 14$ and $g(x) = x^2 + 30$ intersect at the point (a, b). If $a < 0$, what is the value of b?

(A) 22
(B) 28
(C) 30
(D) 39
(E) 46

374. For $0 \leq t \leq 9$, the motion of a particle can be modeled by the function $s(t) = -t^2 + 9t$ where s is the height of the particle in feet at time t seconds. What is the height of the particle at a time of 4 seconds?

(A) 1 foot
(B) 16 feet
(C) 18 feet
(D) 20 feet
(E) 28 feet

375. If the function $f(x) = x^2 - 9x + 8$ is graphed in the (x, y) coordinate plane, then for which of the following values of x will the graph of $f(x)$ be below the x-axis?

(A) $x < 1$
(B) $x < 8$
(C) $x < 1$ and $x > 8$
(D) $1 < x < 8$
(E) The graph is not below the x-axis for any values of x.

376. How many real number solutions does the equation $2x^3 = 9$ have?

(A) 0
(B) 1
(C) 2
(D) 3
(E) 9

377. Based on the following table of values, what is the minimum number of zeros of the function $g(x)$?

x	−5	−3	0	1
$g(x)$	0	0	1	8

(A) 1
(B) 2
(C) 3
(D) 4
(E) Cannot be determined from the given information

378. If $f(m, n) = m^2 - n - 3$ and both m and n are positive numbers, then which of the following statements must be true?

(A) $f(m, n) < -3$
(B) $f(m, n) < 0$
(C) $f(m, n) > -3$
(D) $f(m, n) > 0$
(E) Cannot be determined from the given information

379. If graphed in the (x, y) coordinate plane, which of the following functions would have a graph that does not intersect the x-axis at any point?

(A) $-x^2 + 10$
(B) $-x^2 - 15$
(C) $x^2 - 8$
(D) $x^2 - 4$
(E) x^2

380. The point (q, r) lies on the graph of a function $f(x)$ in the (x, y) coordinate plane. If the graph of $g(x)$ results from shifting the graph of $f(x)$ up 10 units, then which of the following points must lie on the graph of $g(x)$?

(A) $(q + 10, r)$
(B) $(q - 10, r)$
(C) $(q, r + 10)$
(D) $(q, r - 10)$
(E) $(q + 10, r - 10)$

381. If $f(x) = 20$ when $x = 3$, then which of the following expressions is equivalent to $f(x)$ for this value of x?

(A) $17x$
(B) $20x$
(C) $20x - 10$
(D) $10x - 10$
(E) $x + 20$

382. If $f(x) = x + 2$ and $g(x) = x^2 - x - 6$, then which of the following is equivalent to $\dfrac{g(x)}{f(x)}$ for all values of $x \ne -2$?

(A) $x - 12$
(B) $x - 8$
(C) $x - 4$
(D) $x - 3$
(E) $x + 4$

383. Which of the following expressions represents a polynomial with exactly one real root?

(A) $x^2 - 3$
(B) $x^2 - 1$
(C) $x^2 + 1$
(D) $x^2 + 2x + 1$
(E) $x^2 + 3x + 2$

384. If $f(x) = 2x + 6$ and $f(b) = 18$, then $b =$

(A) 6
(B) 12
(C) 24
(D) 36
(E) 42

385. If $x^2 = 8x - 15$, then which of the following is a possible value of x?

    (A) −15

    (B) −8

    (C) −3

    (D) 0

    (E) 5

CHAPTER 7

Preparing for Higher Math: Geometry

Use the following information to answer questions 386–387.

In a track and field competition, a particular track is designed according to the figure below. The inner dimensions of the track have two "straights" of 84 meters joined by two semicircles, each with a radius of 37 meters. For a 6-lane track, the outer semicircle has a radius of 44 meters.

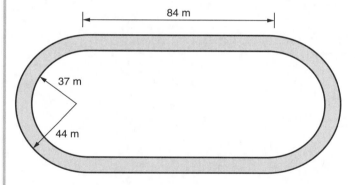

MODELING

386. What is the approximate width of a single lane of the track?

    (A)   1.0 m
    (B)   1.2 m
    (C)   1.5 m
    (D)   3.7 m
    (E)   7.0 m

MODELING **387.** The track itself (shown in the figure with gray) is paved with asphalt, at a cost of $20 per square meter. The inner part of the track will be sodded with grass, which costs $4 per square meter. What is the total cost for the sod and the asphalt, rounded to the nearest thousand?

(A) $45,000
(B) $82,000
(C) $91,000
(D) $101,000
(E) $312,000

388. If the area of the square *ABCD* in the following figure is 16, what is the value of tan *x*?

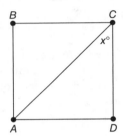

(A) $\dfrac{\sqrt{2}}{8}$

(B) $\dfrac{1}{4}$

(C) 1

(D) $\sqrt{2}$

(E) $4\sqrt{2}$

389. In the standard (*x*, *y*) coordinate plane, what are the coordinates of the midpoint of the line segment connecting (2, 7) and (5, 7)?

(A) (5, 7)
(B) (3.5, 7)
(C) (7, 14)
(D) (3, 0)
(E) (5, 2)

390. In the standard (x, y) coordinate plane, the coordinates of the midpoint of a line segment AB are $(2, 5)$. If the coordinates of the point A are $(1, 0)$, what is the length of the line segment AB?

(A) $\sqrt{2}$

(B) $3\sqrt{3}$

(C) $4\sqrt{3}$

(D) $\sqrt{26}$

(E) $2\sqrt{26}$

391. In the standard (x, y) coordinate plane, at what point does the graph of the line $y - 7x = -10$ cross the y-axis?

(A) $y = -10$
(B) $y = -7$
(C) $y = -3$
(D) $y = 7$
(E) $y = 10$

392. In the following figure, the midpoint of line MN is P, while the midpoint of the line segment QP is R. If the length of QR is 6 and the length of MQ is 4, what is the length of MN?

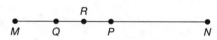

(A) 18
(B) 24
(C) 26
(D) 32
(E) 42

393. In the following figure, lines *m* and *n* are parallel, and the value of *x* is 36. What is the value of *y*?

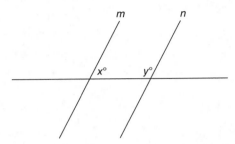

(A) 24
(B) 36
(C) 64
(D) 72F
(E) 144

394. The area of a rectangle in the (*x*, *y*) coordinate plane is 6. The corners of the rectangle are the points *A* (1, 4), *B* (4, 4), *C* (4, 6), and *D* (*x*, *y*). What are the coordinates of point *D*?

(A) (1, 3)
(B) (1, 6)
(C) (4, 1)
(D) (4, 3)
(E) (4, 7)

395. What is the slope of a line that passes through the points $\left(-\dfrac{1}{2}, 2\right)$ and $\left(-\dfrac{1}{4}, \dfrac{1}{4}\right)$ in the (*x*, *y*) coordinate plane?

(A) −28
(B) −10
(C) −7
(D) $-\dfrac{5}{2}$
(E) $-\dfrac{7}{4}$

396. In the following figure, the height of triangle *MNP* is 10 units larger than the height of triangle *ABC*. Both triangles have a base of length *x*. If the area of triangle *ABC* is 50 square units and *x* = 5, what is the area of triangle *MNP* in square units?

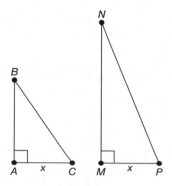

(A) 55
(B) 60
(C) 65
(D) 70
(E) 75

397. The circle in the following figure is centered at the point *O*, and the points *A* and *B* lie on its circumference. In degrees, what is the measure of angle *AOB*?

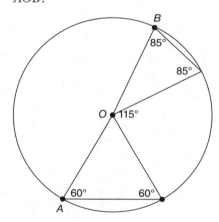

(A) 95
(B) 165
(C) 175
(D) 180
(E) 190

398. Which of the following equations represents a line that is perpendicular to the line $5x - 2y = 8$?

(A) $-2x + 2y = 8$
(B) $5x - 2y = -12$
(C) $2x - 5y = 20$
(D) $-2x + 5y = 11$
(E) $-2x - 5y = 10$

399. A line in the (x, y) coordinate plane has a slope of $-\dfrac{5}{4}$ and passes through the point $(-3, 5)$. What is the y-intercept of this line?

(A) -5
(B) $-\dfrac{15}{4}$
(C) $\dfrac{5}{4}$
(D) 14
(E) 20

400. A line in the (x, y) coordinate plane has a positive y-intercept c and a negative slope. Which of the following statements MUST be true about the x-intercept of this line?

(A) $x < c$
(B) $x < 0$
(C) $x = c$
(D) $x > c$
(E) $x > 0$

401. In the following figure, lines AB and PQ each have a length of 5 units and are parallel to the x-axis. If the coordinates of P are $(3, -2)$, what are the coordinates of Q?

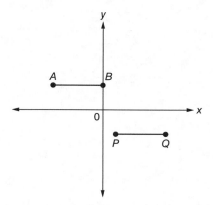

(A) $(-8, -7)$
(B) $(-2, 3)$
(C) $(2, 0)$
(D) $(3, 3)$
(E) $(8, -2)$

402. Which of the following could be the coordinates of the point M in the (x, y) coordinate plane shown?

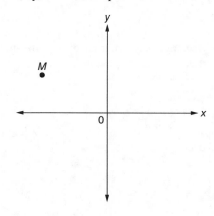

(A) $(-2, -3)$
(B) $(-2, 2)$
(C) $(8, 2)$
(D) $(6, -2)$
(E) $(10, -3)$

403. In the following figure, lines m and n are parallel, and line ℓ is a transversal crossing both lines. If the sum of x and y is 160, what is the value of z?

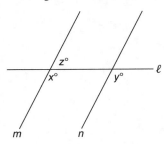

(A) 30
(B) 80
(C) 95
(D) 100
(E) 200

404. In the (x, y) coordinate plane, a circle with radius 6 is centered at point Q on the x-axis. If the point $(-9, 0)$ is on the circumference of the circle, which of the following could be the x-coordinate of Q?

(A) −12
(B) −3
(C) 3
(D) 9
(E) 21

405. In the following figure, $ABCD$ is a rectangle such that $\tan x = \dfrac{8}{3}$. In square feet, what is the area of the rectangle?

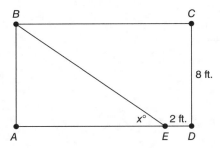

(A) 16
(B) 24
(C) 40
(D) 48
(E) 52

406. Which of the following equations represents the same line as the equation $-2x + 6y = 14$?

(A) $y = -3x$

(B) $y = \dfrac{7}{3}x$

(C) $y = -3x + 7$

(D) $y = \dfrac{1}{3}x + 14$

(E) $y = \dfrac{1}{3}x + \dfrac{7}{3}$

407. A line in the (x, y) coordinate plane is defined such that each y-coordinate is found by multiplying the x-coordinate by 3 and adding 2. What is the y-intercept of this line?

(A) 0

(B) 2

(C) 5

(D) 8

(E) 10

408. In the (x, y) coordinate plane, what is the x-intercept of the line $2x - 5y = 10$?

(A) −5

(B) −2

(C) 2

(D) 5

(E) 10

409. Which of the following statements must be true of a line in the (x, y) coordinate plane defined by the equation $x = c$ for some constant c?

  I. The line is parallel to the y-axis.

  II. The line is perpendicular to the x-axis.

  III. The line has an x- and y-intercept of c.

(A) I only

(B) II only

(C) III only

(D) I and II only

(E) I, II, and III

410. Which of the following is the slope of a line that is parallel to the line that would pass through the points A and B in the figure shown?

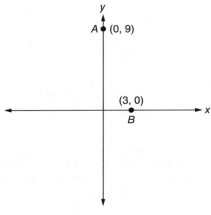

(A) -6

(B) -3

(C) $-\dfrac{1}{3}$

(D) $\dfrac{1}{3}$

(E) 3

411. In the following figure, M is the midpoint of the line segment PQ. What is the value of x?

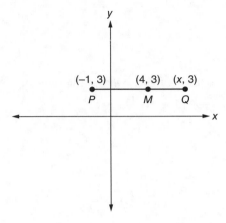

(A) 3
(B) 5
(C) 6
(D) 9
(E) 10

412. The point A lies along the line $7x - 6y = 8$ in the (x, y) coordinate plane. If the x-coordinate of A is 2, what is the y-coordinate?

(A) −6
(B) 1
(C) 3
(D) 8
(E) 14

413. The sides of an equilateral triangle ABC drawn in the (x, y) coordinate plane have sides of length 3. Which of the following pairs of coordinates could represent the endpoints of the line segment AB?

(A) (−3, 2) and (0, 2)
(B) (−1, 4) and (3, 5)
(C) (6, 3) and (10, 13)
(D) (5, 0) and (10, 0)
(E) (8, −3) and (8, 15)

414. If the point $(4, y)$ is on the line $-8x - 4y = 16$, what is the value of y?

   (A) -32
   (B) -18
   (C) -12
   (D) 4
   (E) 14

415. Given the parallelogram in the following figure, what is the value of $x + y$?

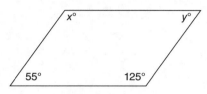

   (A) 55
   (B) 90
   (C) 125
   (D) 180
   (E) 230

416. Given the right triangle in the following figure, what is the value of x?

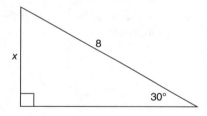

   (A) 4
   (B) $2\sqrt{5}$
   (C) 8
   (D) $4\sqrt{3}$
   (E) $8\sqrt{3}$

417. A line segment AB in the (x, y) coordinate plane has a midpoint that lies on the y-axis and is perpendicular to that axis. If the coordinates of point A are $(-8, 6)$, which of the following could be the coordinates of point B?

(A) $(-10, 8)$
(B) $(-8, -6)$
(C) $(-4, 3)$
(D) $(4, 6)$
(E) $(8, 6)$

418. In the following figure, the equation of line m is $y = \dfrac{3}{2}x + 1$, and line n, which is parallel to the x-axis, intersects the y-axis at the point A $(0, 8)$. If lines m and n intersect at point B, what is the x-coordinate of point B?

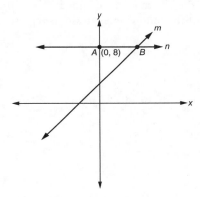

(A) $\dfrac{2}{3}$

(B) 1

(C) $\dfrac{14}{3}$

(D) 8

(E) 13

419. Which of the following is the equation of a line parallel to the line passing through the points $(-1, 4)$ and $(3, 8)$?

(A) $y = x - 10$

(B) $y = 2x + 7$

(C) $y = -x + 4$

(D) $y = -\dfrac{1}{2}x - 6$

(E) $y = \dfrac{1}{3}x - 8$

420. The sides of the rhombus $ABCD$ in the following figure all have the same length, and the diagonal AC is half the length of the diagonal BD. If the length of diagonal AC is m, which of the following expressions represents the area of $ABCD$ in terms of m?

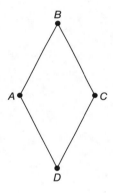

(A) $\dfrac{3}{2}m$

(B) m^2

(C) $\dfrac{1}{2}m^2$

(D) $\dfrac{\sqrt{3}}{2}m^2$

(E) $\dfrac{3}{2}m^2$

421. Each of the following equations represents a line in the (x, y) coordinate plane EXCEPT

(A) $y = \dfrac{x}{4}$

(B) $7x - 5x = \dfrac{1}{2}$

(C) $y = \dfrac{x - 3}{5}$

(D) $y = x(x + 1)$

(E) $\dfrac{y}{2} = \dfrac{x}{9}$

422. The points M, N, P, and Q lie on a line in that order such that N is the midpoint of the line segment MP. If the length of MN is 14, the length of NP is $2x$, and the length of PQ is $4x - 9$, what is the length of the line segment MQ?

(A) 7
(B) 19
(C) 21
(D) 33
(E) 47

423. If the point $(2m, m - 1)$ lies on the line $y = x + 4$ in the (x, y) coordinate plane, then $m =$

(A) −5
(B) −1
(C) 3
(D) 5
(E) 7

424. Every point on a line in the (x, y) coordinate plane has the form $\left(x, \dfrac{x - 1}{4}\right)$. Which of the following is the equation of this line in standard form?

(A) $y - 4x = -1$
(B) $4y - x = -1$
(C) $4y - x = 4$
(D) $4y - 4x = 4$
(E) $4y - 4x = 1$

425. The distance between points P and Q in the (x, y) coordinate plane is half the distance between $(-4, 2)$ and $(-8, 1)$. What is the distance between points P and Q?

(A) $\dfrac{\sqrt{15}}{2}$

(B) $\dfrac{\sqrt{17}}{2}$

(C) $\dfrac{\sqrt{45}}{2}$

(D) $\sqrt{34}$

(E) $3\sqrt{10}$

426. What is the slope of the line in the following figure?

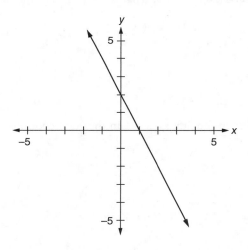

(A) -3
(B) -2
(C) $-\dfrac{1}{2}$

(D) $\dfrac{1}{2}$

(E) 2

427. In the (x, y) coordinate plane, which of the following points would lie on the graph of the line $2y - x = 8$?

(A) $(-2, -3)$
(B) $(-1, 1)$
(C) $(0, 4)$
(D) $(2, 3)$
(E) $(4, 8)$

Use the following information to answer questions 428–429.

The Great Pyramid of Giza was constructed around 2560 BC in Egypt and is the only one of the Seven Wonders of the Ancient World that is still intact. As seen in the following diagram, the pyramid has a square base with side lengths of 230 meters, and it has a vertical height of 147 meters.

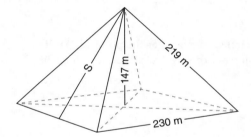

MODELING **428.** The line marked "s" intersects the base of the pyramid at a right angle. What is the length of line "s" rounded to the nearest meter?

(A) 187 meters
(B) 219 meters
(C) 230 meters
(D) 253 meters
(E) 273 meters

MODELING **429.** The four triangular surfaces of the pyramid were originally covered with limestone blocks with approximate dimensions of 3 meters by 4 meters and 1 meter thick. Each stone weighed approximately 40 tons. What was the approximate weight of all the limestone blocks used to cover the pyramid, rounded to the nearest thousand tons?

(A) 72,000 tons
(B) 153,000 tons
(C) 211,000 tons
(D) 225,000 tons
(E) 287,000 tons

430. In the (x, y) coordinate plane, the lines $y = 5x - 1$ and $y = -3x - 17$ intersect at the point with coordinates

(A) $(-9, -46)$
(B) $(-8, -41)$
(C) $(-2, -11)$
(D) $(2, 9)$
(E) $(8, 39)$

431. In the (x, y) coordinate plane, a circle is centered at the point $(2, 5)$. If the point $(4, 9)$ is on the circumference of this circle, then which of the following distances is the radius?

(A) 2
(B) 4
(C) $2\sqrt{5}$
(D) $\sqrt{34}$
(E) $4\sqrt{5}$

432. For the triangle shown in the following figure, what is the value of sin x?

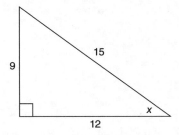

(A) $\dfrac{3}{5}$

(B) $\dfrac{3}{4}$

(C) $\dfrac{4}{5}$

(D) $\dfrac{4}{3}$

(E) $\dfrac{7}{3}$

433. If $0° \le \alpha \le 90°$ and $\cos \alpha = \dfrac{9}{7}$, then $\sec \alpha =$

(A) $-\dfrac{9}{7}$

(B) $-\dfrac{7}{9}$

(C) $\dfrac{1}{8}$

(D) $\dfrac{2}{7}$

(E) $\dfrac{7}{9}$

434. In square units, what is the area of an equilateral triangle with sides of length 6 units?

(A) 18

(B) 36

(C) $9\sqrt{3}$

(D) $3\sqrt{5}$

(E) $18\sqrt{5}$

435. In the following figure, triangle ABC is a right triangle such that the sine of angle B is $\dfrac{3}{4}$. What is the value of x?

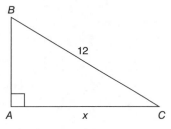

(A) 4

(B) 6

(C) 9

(D) 12

(E) 16

436. In the following figure, the area of the circle centered at the point O is $\dfrac{29\pi}{4}$ square feet. Given that AB has a length of 2 feet, what is the area of triangle ABC in square feet?

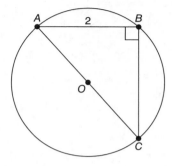

(A) 1

(B) $\dfrac{\sqrt{13}}{2}$

(C) 5

(D) 10

(E) $4\sqrt{29}$

437. In the (x, y) coordinate plane, which of the following is an equation of the circle with a center at the point $(0, -5)$ and a radius of 2?

(A) $x^2 + (y+5)^2 = 4$

(B) $(x+5)^2 + y^2 = 16$

(C) $(x+5)^2 + (y+5)^2 = 4$

(D) $(x-5)^2 + (y-5)^2 = 4$

(E) $x^2 + (y-5)^2 = 16$

438. In the following figure, the length of *PR* is half the length of *QR*. What is the length of line segment *PQ*?

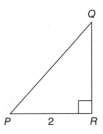

(A) $\sqrt{2}$

(B) $\sqrt{5}$

(C) $2\sqrt{2}$

(D) $2\sqrt{5}$

(E) $4\sqrt{5}$

439. The length of one leg of a right triangle is three times as large as the length of the other leg. If the hypotenuse has a length of 10 inches, which of the following is the perimeter of the triangle in inches?

(A) $\sqrt{10}$

(B) $4\sqrt{10}$

(C) 10

(D) $10+\sqrt{10}$

(E) $10+4\sqrt{10}$

440. Which of the following expressions represents the circumference of a circle with a radius of *x*?

(A) $2x$
(B) πx
(C) $2x\pi$
(D) $4x\pi$
(E) $4x$

441. In the following figure, what is the value of cos x?

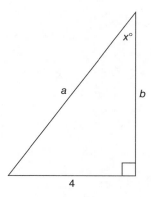

(A) $\dfrac{b}{a}$

(B) $\dfrac{a}{b}$

(C) $\dfrac{4}{a}$

(D) $\dfrac{b}{4}$

(E) $\dfrac{a}{4}$

442. In the (x, y) coordinate plane, the points A (6, 0) and B (6, 10) are on the circumference of a circle such that the line AB is a diameter of the circle. Which of the following is an equation representing the described circle?

(A) $(x-6)^2 + (y-5)^2 = 25$

(B) $(x-6)^2 + (y-5)^2 = 100$

(C) $(x-6)^2 + (y-10)^2 = 25$

(D) $(x-6)^2 + (y-10)^2 = 100$

(E) $(x-5)^2 + (y-10)^2 = 100$

443. In the following figure, the square $ABCD$ is inscribed in the circle centered at point O. What is the area of the circle?

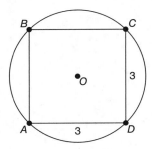

(A) $\dfrac{\pi}{4}$

(B) $\dfrac{3\pi}{4}$

(C) $\dfrac{3\pi}{2}$

(D) $\dfrac{9\pi}{4}$

(E) $\dfrac{9\pi}{2}$

444. If a right triangle has legs of length $5x$ and x, which of the following expressions represents the length of its hypotenuse in terms of x?

(A) $2x$

(B) $5x$

(C) $x\sqrt{6}$

(D) $2x\sqrt{6}$

(E) $x\sqrt{26}$

445. In square centimeters, what is the area of the parallelogram in the following figure?

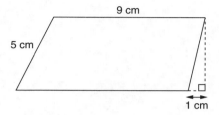

(A) $18\sqrt{6}$

(B) 45

(C) $\dfrac{95}{2}$

(D) $20\sqrt{6}$

(E) 50

446. In the following figure, *ABC* is an equilateral triangle. What is the value of *x*?

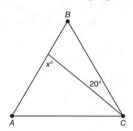

(A) 40

(B) 60

(C) 80

(D) 100

(E) 120

447. A circle in the (*x, y*) coordinate plane is determined by the equation $(x-8)^2 + (y-10)^2 = 4$. Which of the following points lies on the circumference of this circle?

(A) (2, 10)

(B) (6, 10)

(C) (8, 6)

(D) (8, 14)

(E) (12, 10)

448. Given the triangle in the following figure, if $\tan x = \dfrac{1}{2}$, then $\sin x =$

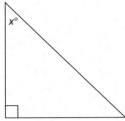

(A) $\sqrt{2}$

(B) $\sqrt{3}$

(C) $\sqrt{5}$

(D) $\dfrac{\sqrt{5}}{5}$

(E) $\dfrac{\sqrt{3}}{2}$

449. If the circumference of a circle is larger than x, then the circle's radius must be larger than

(A) 2π

(B) $2\pi x$

(C) $x - 2\pi$

(D) $\dfrac{x}{2\pi}$

(E) $\dfrac{1}{2\pi}$

450. The half circle pictured is centered at the point A and has a radius of 2 meters. In meters, what is the length of the arc PQ?

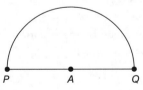

(A) π

(B) 2π

(C) 4π

(D) 8π

(E) 16π

Preparing for Higher Math: Statistics and Probability

Use the following information to answer questions 451–453.

The eye color of 200 students in a high school was observed and recorded in the bar graph below.

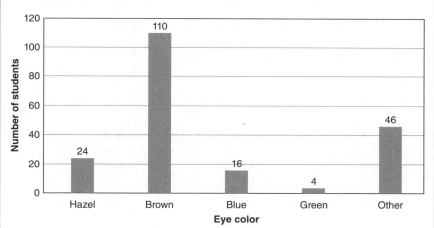

MODELING **451.** If a person in this sample were randomly selected, what is the probability that this person has blue or green eyes?

(A) $\dfrac{1}{5}$

(B) $\dfrac{1}{10}$

(C) $\dfrac{2}{25}$

(D) $\dfrac{1}{50}$

(E) $\dfrac{11}{20}$

MODELING **452.** How many additional hazel-eyed students must be added to the population so that there would be a $\dfrac{1}{2}$ probability of selecting a hazel-eyed student from the new population in a random drawing?

(A) 24
(B) 48
(C) 56
(D) 152
(E) 212

MODELING **453.** The names of all the students who do *not* have brown eyes were entered into a random drawing. What's the probability that a student with hazel eyes will be chosen in the drawing?

(A) $\dfrac{22}{25}$

(B) $\dfrac{33}{100}$

(C) $\dfrac{3}{25}$

(D $\dfrac{4}{15}$

(E) $\dfrac{11}{15}$

MODELING **454.** A 6-sided dice is rolled twice. What is the probability that a 5 will be the outcome of the first roll and a 6 will be the outcome of the second roll?

(A) $\dfrac{1}{3}$

(B) $\dfrac{1}{6}$

(C) $\dfrac{1}{18}$

(D) $\dfrac{1}{30}$

(E) $\dfrac{1}{36}$

MODELING **455.** Sixty percent of the 250-member junior class at Central High School took the ACT. Half of that test-taking group chose to take the essay portion. How many Central High School juniors took the essay portion of the ACT?

(A) 25
(B) 30
(C) 50
(D) 75
(E) 150

456. A student has 5 different shirts, 3 different pairs of pants, and 2 different pairs of shoes in his closet. Without concern for fashion faux pas, how many different outfit combinations (one shirt, one pair of pants, and one pair of shoes) are possible?

(A) 10
(B) 15
(C) 20
(D) 25
(E) 30

MODELING **457.** Two classes took the math final exam. The first class had 20 students and averaged 82%. The second class had 26 students and averaged and 86%. What is the exam average of both classes combined?

(A) 83.9
(B) 84.0
(C) 84.1
(D) 84.3
(E) 84.5

458. A game's card set is made up of 6 blue cards and 9 red cards. If a player randomly selects one of these cards, what is the probability the selected card will be blue?

(A) $\dfrac{1}{15}$

(B) $\dfrac{1}{6}$

(C) $\dfrac{2}{5}$

(D) $\dfrac{3}{5}$

(E) $\dfrac{2}{3}$

459. In a geometric series, the ratio of any term to the following term is constant. What is the next term in the series $2, 3, \dfrac{9}{2}, \ldots$?

(A) $\dfrac{27}{4}$

(B) $\dfrac{9}{4}$

(C) 3

(D) $\dfrac{9}{2}$

(E) $\dfrac{27}{2}$

460. The value of a number x is twice the value of y, and the average of the two numbers is 30. What is the value of x?

(A) 30
(B) 40
(C) 60
(D) 120
(E) 140

MODELING **461.** A retailer's website allows shoppers to customize the shoes they order. Customers may select one of 3 different colors, one of 2 types of laces, and one of 8 special logos. With these choices, how many different shoe designs are possible?

(A) 14
(B) 16
(C) 36
(D) 48
(E) 52

462. Two 6-sided dice will be rolled together. What is the probability that one die will be a 5 and the other a 6?

(A) $\dfrac{1}{3}$

(B) $\dfrac{1}{6}$

(C) $\dfrac{1}{18}$

(D) $\dfrac{1}{30}$

(E) $\dfrac{1}{36}$

463. There are twice as many red pens as there are blue pens in a desk. If a pen is randomly selected, what is the probability it is blue?

(A) $\dfrac{1}{4}$

(B) $\dfrac{1}{3}$

(C) $\dfrac{2}{3}$

(D) $\dfrac{1}{2}$

(E) Cannot be determined from the given information

464. The probability of randomly selecting a green marble from a bag is $\dfrac{4}{5}$. If there are 110 marbles in the bag, how many are NOT green?

(A) 20
(B) 22
(C) 36
(D) 80
(E) 88

465. Which of the following statements is true of $P(A)$, that is, the probability of A, for any event A?

 I. If A is very likely to occur, $P(A) > 1$
 II. $P(A) = 1 - P(A \text{ not occurring})$
 III. $P(A) \geq 0$

(A) I only
(B) II only
(C) III only
(D) I and II only
(E) II and III only

466. If the sum of n numbers is m and the average of the same n numbers is p, what is the value of n in terms of m and p?

(A) $\dfrac{p}{m}$

(B) $\dfrac{m}{p}$

(C) mp

(D) $m + p$

(E) $m - p$

467. The tenth term of an arithmetic sequence is 38, and the second term is 6. What is the value of the first term of this sequence?

(A) 0
(B) 2
(C) 4
(D) 14
(E) 26

468. How many different arrangements of the letters A, D, G, and F are possible?

(A) 10
(B) 16
(C) 24
(D) 256
(E) 325

469. A fair coin is flipped five times, and each flip results in tails. What is the probability the coin will land on tails on the sixth flip?

(A) $\dfrac{1}{64}$

(B) $\dfrac{1}{10}$

(C) $\dfrac{1}{7}$

(D) $\dfrac{1}{6}$

(E) $\dfrac{1}{2}$

470. What is the 35th term of the sequence −1, 5, −2, 1, 5, 2, … ?

    (A) −2
    (B) −1
    (C) 1
    (D) 2
    (E) 5

471. A number is randomly selected from all integers between 1 and 25 inclusive. What is the probability the selected number is prime?

    (A) $\dfrac{1}{10}$

    (B) $\dfrac{1}{9}$

    (C) $\dfrac{9}{25}$

    (D) $\dfrac{2}{5}$

    (E) $\dfrac{12}{25}$

472. The probabilities for 5 events are listed in the following table. Which event is the LEAST likely to occur?

Event	Probability
Event 1	0.25
Event 2	0.35
Event 3	0.47
Event 4	0.40
Event 5	0.29

    (A) Event 1
    (B) Event 2
    (C) Event 3
    (D) Event 4
    (E) Event 5

MODELING 473. Two contest winners are chosen by having their names drawn out of a hat one at a time. Once a name is drawn, it is not replaced, and each person is allowed only one entry. In total, 7 people entered the contest. If Sara's name was not chosen on the first draw, what is the probability it will be chosen on the second?

(A) $\dfrac{1}{7}$

(B) $\dfrac{1}{6}$

(C) $\dfrac{2}{7}$

(D) $\dfrac{2}{5}$

(E) $\dfrac{5}{6}$

474. In a game, a complete set of cards consists of one situational card, one power card, and one level card. If Blake holds 5 situational cards, 4 power cards, and 10 level cards, how many different complete sets of cards does he have?

(A) 9
(B) 19
(C) 30
(D) 131
(E) 200

475. The average of a set of six numbers is 10. If 5 is added to each number in the set, what is the average of the new set of numbers?

(A) 5
(B) 15
(C) 20
(D) 50
(E) 80

MODELING **476.** Hanna and Jake are hoping to get selected as the host of this year's talent show. The committee chooses a host by random selection, and this year only 29 students entered their name into the drawing. What is the probability either Hanna or Jake is selected as the host this year?

(A) $\dfrac{1}{841}$

(B) $\dfrac{2}{841}$

(C) $\dfrac{1}{58}$

(D) $\dfrac{1}{29}$

(E) $\dfrac{2}{29}$

477. A set of numbers contains m numbers, one of which is even. If a number is randomly selected from the set, what is the probability it is NOT even?

(A) $\dfrac{1}{m}$

(B) $\dfrac{1}{m-1}$

(C) $\dfrac{1}{m+1}$

(D) $\dfrac{m-1}{m}$

(E) $\dfrac{m}{m+1}$

478. Two 6-sided dice are rolled together. What is the probability that the sum of the two numbers is 3?

(A) $\dfrac{1}{6}$

(B) $\dfrac{1}{9}$

(C) $\dfrac{1}{18}$

(D) $\dfrac{1}{24}$

(E) $\dfrac{1}{36}$

MODELING **479.** A governing committee of 3 is chosen out of 30 people. The committee consists of a president, a treasurer, and a vice president. Only one person may be selected for any given position. Which of the following expressions represents the number of possible combinations of people who could serve in the 3 positions on the governing committee?

(A) 3×30

(B) 30^3

(C) $30^3 \times 29^2 \times 28$

(D) $30 \times 29 \times 28$

(E) $30 + 29 + 28$

480. If the sum of 10 numbers is x, which of the following expressions represents the average of these 10 numbers?

(A) $\dfrac{x}{10}$

(B) x^{10}

(C) $10x$

(D) $x + 10$

(E) $10 - x$

481. Three telephones in a shipment of 8 are known to be defective. A randomly selected telephone is removed from the shipment and tested. It is found not to be defective. If a second telephone is randomly selected from those remaining, what is the probability of it NOT being defective?

(A) $\dfrac{1}{4}$

(B) $\dfrac{4}{7}$

(C) $\dfrac{1}{3}$

(D) $\dfrac{3}{8}$

(E) $\dfrac{3}{7}$

482. An urn contains 5 white marbles and 6 green marbles. Which of the following would INCREASE the probability of randomly selecting a white marble from this urn?

    I. Increasing the number of white marbles only
   II. Increasing the number of green marbles only
  III. Decreasing the number of white marbles and green marbles by the same number

(A) I only
(B) II only
(C) III only
(D) I and II only
(E) I and III only

483. A coin is selected from a box containing two different types of coins. The probability of selecting the first type of coin is three times the probability of selecting the second type. If there are 240 coins of the first type, how many coins of the second type are in the box?

(A) 80
(B) 110
(C) 243
(D) 720
(E) 832

484. The median of a list of 7 distinct numbers is 3. If a number $x > 3$ is included in the list, which of the following will be true of the new list?

(A) The median will be zero.
(B) The median will be smaller than three, but not zero.
(C) The median will remain three.
(D) The median will be larger than three.
(E) The median will be larger than x.

485. How many distinct arrangements of 4 letters (without repeats) from the set {A, B, C, D, E} are possible?

(A) 15
(B) 20
(C) 25
(D) 120
(E) 625

486. If $x = 7$, what is the probability a randomly selected number from the set $\{x - 5, 2x + 4, -x, x + 5, x + 3\}$ will be even?

(A) 0

(B) $\dfrac{1}{5}$

(C) $\dfrac{2}{5}$

(D) $\dfrac{3}{5}$

(E) $\dfrac{4}{5}$

487. If the median of 1, x, y, 4, and z is x, and $y > z > 4$, which of the following statements MUST be true?

(A) $x < 1$
(B) $x < 4$
(C) $x < z$
(D) $1 < x < 4$
(E) $y < x < z$

MODELING **488.** Aiden's work schedule for the week is represented in the following table. If this schedule remains the same for 4 weeks, and if a day from the 4-week schedule is selected at random, what is the probability that the day selected is a day when Aiden is scheduled to work?

Day	Schedule
Monday	Off duty
Tuesday	8 A.M.–12 noon
Wednesday	8 A.M.–12 noon
Thursday	Off duty
Friday	Off duty
Saturday	4 P.M.–8 P.M.
Sunday	4 P.M.–8 P.M.

(A) $\dfrac{1}{28}$

(B) $\dfrac{1}{7}$

(C) $\dfrac{3}{7}$

(D) $\dfrac{4}{7}$

(E) $\dfrac{5}{7}$

MODELING **489.** On an exam, students must select one short-answer question and one essay question to complete. If the exam has 5 short-answer and 3 essay questions, how many distinct combinations of questions can students select?

(A) 2
(B) 7
(C) 8
(D) 15
(E) 45

490. The average of 4 consecutive integers is 14.5. What is the sum of the largest and the smallest of the integers?

(A) 3
(B) 23
(C) 27
(D) 29
(E) 31

491. If the probability of event A occurring is 0.4 and the probability of event B occurring is 0.2, which of the following probabilities must be greater than 0.5? Assume that events A and B cannot occur at the same time.

   I. The probability of event A not occurring
  II. The probability of event B not occurring
 III. The probability of either event A or event B occurring

(A) I only
(B) II only
(C) III only
(D) I and II only
(E) I, II, and III

492. A box contains red and black cards. The probability of selecting a red card is half the probability of selecting a black card. What is the probability of selecting a black card?

(A) $\dfrac{1}{4}$

(B) $\dfrac{1}{3}$

(C) $\dfrac{1}{2}$

(D) $\dfrac{2}{3}$

(E) $\dfrac{3}{4}$

493. Which of the following could NOT represent the probability of an event occurring?

(A) $\dfrac{1}{1056}$

(B) $\dfrac{5}{18}$

(C) $\dfrac{59}{61}$

(D) $\dfrac{57}{41}$

(E) $\dfrac{6}{257}$

494. One of 3 cards must be selected to continue a game. The probability the first card will be selected is $\dfrac{2}{5}$, while the probability the second card will be selected is $\dfrac{1}{8}$. What is the probability the third card will be selected?

(A) $\dfrac{1}{13}$

(B) $\dfrac{1}{5}$

(C) $\dfrac{19}{40}$

(D) $\dfrac{29}{40}$

(E) $\dfrac{12}{13}$

495. What is the median of the data list q, x, y, z, w if the inequality $y < x < w < 8 < z < q$ is true?

(A) q
(B) x
(C) y
(D) z
(E) w

496. The list of numbers 1,1, x, y, 10, 14 is written in order of smallest to largest. If the median of the list is 5, which of the following numbers is a possible value of the product xy?

(A) 8
(B) 17
(C) 20
(D) 24
(E) 29

MODELING) **497.** In a department store, there are x items on sale at a discount. If a total of 171 items are on sale at the store and the probability an item is not on sale at a discount is $\dfrac{2}{3}$, what is the value of x?

(A) 55
(B) 57
(C) 112
(D) 114
(E) 118

498. Hunter has collected 35 science books over the last two years, and 5 of these science books cover biology. What is the probability a randomly selected science book in his collection covers biology?

(A) $\dfrac{1}{35}$

(B) $\dfrac{1}{30}$

(C) $\dfrac{1}{7}$

(D) $\dfrac{1}{6}$

(E) $\dfrac{1}{5}$

MODELING **499.** The results of a career interest survey of students in a statewide mathematics club are provided in the following table. If a student is randomly selected from this group, what is the probability the student indicated interest in an aviation career?

Career	Number of Students
Medical (doctor, nurse, etc.)	82
Aviation	18
Engineering	22
Computer science and technology	48
Other	30

(A) $\dfrac{1}{200}$

(B) $\dfrac{1}{182}$

(C) $\dfrac{1}{18}$

(D) $\dfrac{9}{100}$

(E) $\dfrac{41}{100}$

500. If the probability of selecting a gray hat from a bin containing gray and black hats is x, which of the following probabilities MUST have a value of $1 - x$?

(A) The probability of selecting two gray hats
(B) The probability of selecting a black hat
(C) The probability of selecting two black hats
(D) The probability of selecting a black hat followed by a gray hat
(E) The probability of selecting a gray hat followed by a black hat

ANSWERS

Chapter 1

1. (C) A percentage is a "part" out of the "whole." In this case, that is $\dfrac{120}{500} = 0.24$, or 24%.

2. (E) Freshmen make up $\dfrac{125}{500} = \dfrac{1}{4}$ of the students. Therefore, since a circle has a total of 360 degrees, the portion of the circle graph that would represent this would have a degree measure of $\dfrac{1}{4}(360) = 90$.

3. (D) A total of 20 students received an A or a B in the course out of a total of $5 + 15 + 20 + 3 + 2 = 45$ students. Therefore, the fraction of those who received an A or a B is $\dfrac{20}{45} = \dfrac{4}{9}$.

4. (C) If there are 1000 students in the school, then there are $0.45 \times 1000 = 450$ freshmen and $0.10 \times 1000 = 100$ juniors. Therefore, the difference is $450 - 100 = 350$.

5. (D) There are four 15-minute periods every hour. Therefore, there are fourteen 15-minute periods in $3\dfrac{1}{2}$ hours. Finally, $14 \times 100 = 1400$.

6. (B) Let x represent the number of text messages sent by the customer during the billing period. The bill's total can be expressed as $45 + 0.15x = 61.50$, which has a solution of $x = 110$.

7. (E) As an equation, the ratio is written as $\dfrac{x}{y} = \dfrac{5}{12}$. If $x = 45$, then this is nine times larger than 5, so $y = 12 \times 9 = 108$.

8. (C) One hour and 20 minutes is equivalent to 80 minutes. At 60 miles per hour, the vehicle is moving at 1 mile per minute and will therefore cover 80 miles.

9. (D) $M\%$ can be written as $\dfrac{M}{100}$, giving us the equation $\dfrac{M}{100}(135) = 54$ or $1.35M = 54$, which has a solution of $M = \dfrac{54}{1.35} = 40$.

10. (B) Let F represent the number of full-time employees and P represent the number of part-time employees. Since there are 800 employees, $F + P = 800$. Also, given the ratio $\dfrac{F}{P} = \dfrac{3}{2}$, we can cross multiply and solve for F: $3P = 2F$, and $F = \dfrac{3}{2}P$. Finally, substitute this value of F into the first equation, and solve for P: $F + P = \dfrac{3}{2}P + P = \dfrac{5}{2}P = 800$, and $P = 800\left(\dfrac{2}{5}\right) = 320$.

11. (C) If one side of the square is x, then the perimeter is $4x$. If we increase x by 20%, the new length of a side will be $1.2x$, and the perimeter will be $4.8x$. The percent increase is then $100\left(\dfrac{4.8x - 4x}{4x}\right) = 100\left(\dfrac{0.8x}{4x}\right) = 20\%$.

12. (C) Stated as equations, the information provided says $0.05x = y$ and $0.25y = z$. Substituting the value of y from the first equation into the second, $0.25(0.05x) = z$, which simplifies to $0.0125x = z$. Solving for x, divide both sides by 0.0125, so $x = 80z$.

13. (C) Let x represent the area of the largest section, y the area of the middle section, and z the area of the smallest section. We will find the largest area first, since it is easiest to work with. Given the total area, $x + y + z = 1550$. Also, given the ratios $2x = 3y$ and $2x = 5z$, we can solve these equations for y and z, respectively: $y = \dfrac{2}{3}x$ and $z = \dfrac{2}{5}x$. Our original equation can now be written as $x + \dfrac{2}{3}x + \dfrac{2}{5}x = 1550$. Collecting terms, $\dfrac{31}{15}x = 1550$, and $x = 750$. The smallest section, z, will have an area of $\dfrac{2}{5}(750) = 300$.

14. (B) The ratio of BA to ED is 4:1, so $x = \dfrac{30}{4} = 7.5$.

15. (E) If a is directly proportional to $\dfrac{b}{2}$, then for some constant k, $a = k(b/2)$. Plugging in $a = 1$ and $b = 10$, we can write $1 = k(10/2)$, and thus $k = 1/5$. Plugging in this value of k into the equation above, we get $a = (1/5)(b/2)$ or $a = b/10$. The final step is to plug in $b = 35$ into this last expression, so $a = (35/10) = 7/2$.

16. (C) $0.8(x + 1) = 2$ is equivalent to $0.8x = 2 - 0.8 = 1.2$, and $x = \dfrac{1.2}{0.8} = 1.5$.

17. (A) The document will contain a total of $500n$ words, since this is the number of pages multiplied by the number of words per page. Since Greg can read w words per minute, he will need $\dfrac{500n}{w}$ minutes to read it.

18. (B) First restate each term as a decimal: $\dfrac{1}{2}\% = 0.5\% = 0.005$, and $\dfrac{1}{20} = 0.05$. Therefore, $\dfrac{1}{2}\%$ of $\dfrac{1}{20}$ is $0.005(0.05) = 0.00025$.

19. (D) Party B received 46% of the votes, so $0.46x = 874$, where x is the total number of votes. Solve for x to find the total: $x = \dfrac{874}{0.46} = 1900$.

20. (D) The area of square A is $3 \times 3 = 9$, and the area of square B is $9 \times 9 = 81$. The ratio 9:81 is equivalent to 1:9.

21. (A) If x is the next largest side, then $\dfrac{2}{x} = \dfrac{4}{12}$ and $x = 6$. If y is the largest side, then $\dfrac{2}{y} = \dfrac{4}{14}$ and $y = 7$. Therefore, the perimeter is $2 + 6 + 7 = 15$.

22. (D) To determine this answer, you must divide the number of math majors (490) by the total number of students (14,000), and then multiply the amount by 100 to get the percentage: $100\left(\dfrac{490}{14,000}\right) = 3.5$.

23. (E) Given the ratio, $\dfrac{AB}{18} = \dfrac{2}{3}$, and $AB = 12$. Since C is the midpoint of DF, $DF = 2(12) = 24$. Finally, the area is $\dfrac{1}{2}(24)(18) = 216$.

24. (B) Since $10FG = BC$, $(1/10)AB = FE$, and $FE = 1$. Therefore, the perimeter is $1 + 3 + 1 + 3 = 8$.

25. (B) For some k, $x = \dfrac{1}{k}y$. Using the values given, $12 = \dfrac{1}{k}(48)$, which means $k = 4$. Therefore, when $y = 12$, $x = \dfrac{1}{4}(12) = 3$.

26. (B) 40% is half of 80%, so 40% of the number is $\dfrac{122}{2} = 61$.

27. (E) $\left(\dfrac{40 \text{ min.}}{28 \text{ hard drives}}\right)(196 \text{ hard drives}) = 7(40) \text{ min.} = 280 \text{ min.}$

28. (C) Expressing the given ratios as equations, $\dfrac{A}{B} = \dfrac{3}{8}$ and $\dfrac{B}{C} = \dfrac{1}{6}$. Solving for B in the second equation, $6B = C$ and $B = \dfrac{C}{6}$. When we substitute this value of B in the first equation, we find $\dfrac{A}{\left(\dfrac{C}{6}\right)} = \dfrac{6A}{C} = \dfrac{3}{8}$. Dividing both sides by 6, $\dfrac{A}{C} = \dfrac{3}{48} = \dfrac{1}{16}$.

29. (C) $(1 - 0.15)(154.99) = 0.85(154.99) = 131.74$

30. (A) If the width is w, then the length is $1.4w$. Since the area of a rectangle is length times width, the area is: $w(1.4w) = 1.4w^2 = 140$. Solving this equation, $w^2 = \dfrac{140}{1.4} = 100$, and $w = 10$.

31. (B) $\dfrac{x}{100}\left(\dfrac{3}{4}\right) = \dfrac{3x}{400}$

32. (B) Convert the fractions to decimals and solve: $0.0025(0.25) = 0.000625$.

33. (B) The total percentage must be 100, so $x = 100 - (35 + 20 + 24) = 21$.

34. (D) When $x = 12$, $\dfrac{12}{y} = \dfrac{1}{6}$ and $y = 72$. The difference is $72 - 12 = 60$.

35. (C) Given the ratio of x to y, $4x = y$, and the area of the larger triangle is $\dfrac{1}{2}(AB)(x+y) = \dfrac{1}{2}(AB)(x+4x) = \dfrac{1}{2}(AB)(5x)$. The area of the smaller triangle is $\dfrac{1}{2}(AB)(x)$, or $\dfrac{1}{5}$ as large. Therefore, the ratio of the areas is 1:5.

36. (E) The length of QP is four times the length of BA. Since the rectangles are similar, this implies $4(13) = x - 13$, or $52 = x - 13$. Therefore, $x = 65$.

37. (B) Given that $0.95(3x) = 39.9$, dividing both sides yields $x = \dfrac{39.9}{0.95(3)} = 14$.

38. (D) The radius is half the diameter, so the area of the circle centered at point O is $\pi\left(\dfrac{AB}{2}\right)^2 = \dfrac{\pi}{4}(AB)^2$. Using the given ratio, $AB = 3CD$, so $CD = \dfrac{AB}{3}$, and the area of the circle centered at P is $\pi\left(\dfrac{CD}{2}\right)^2 = \dfrac{\pi}{4}(CD)^2 = \dfrac{\pi}{4}\left(\dfrac{AB}{3}\right)^2 = \dfrac{\pi}{36}(AB)^2$. The ratio of the two areas is then $\dfrac{\dfrac{\pi}{4}(AB)^2}{\dfrac{\pi}{36}(AB)^2} = \dfrac{\pi}{4}\left(\dfrac{36}{\pi}\right) = \dfrac{36}{4}$, which we see is equivalent to 9:1.

39. (C) Let A be the area of the square and s be the length of one side. We are told that $s = 0.2A$; since this is a square, $A = s^2$ and $s = 0.2s^2$. Bringing all the terms to one side and factoring, we have $s(0.2s - 1) = 0$. The solutions are $s = 0$ and $s = \dfrac{1}{0.2} = 5$. The sides can't have a length of zero, so each side has a length of 5, and the perimeter is $4 \times 5 = 20$.

40. (B) Assuming x and y are nonzero, we can write $\dfrac{x}{y} = \dfrac{2}{5}$ and $y = 0.3z$. Using substitution, $\dfrac{x}{y} = \dfrac{2}{5} = \dfrac{x}{0.3z}$ and $\dfrac{x}{z} = \dfrac{2(0.3)}{5} = \dfrac{0.6}{5} = \dfrac{6}{50} = \dfrac{3}{25}$.

41. (B) Taking $x\%$ of something is the same as multiplying by $\dfrac{x}{100}$. Therefore, if $\dfrac{x}{50}(280) = 112$, then to find $x\%$ of 280, we multiply both sides by $\dfrac{1}{2}$ to get $\dfrac{1}{2}\left(\dfrac{x}{50}\right)(280) = \dfrac{1}{2}(112)$. This is equivalent to $\dfrac{x}{100}(280) = 56$.

42. (C) The length of AC is three times larger than the length of DF. Since the triangles are similar, this pattern will be true for each pair of sides. Further, since the triangles are isosceles, $BC = AB = x$, and $ED = EF = \dfrac{x}{3}$. The perimeter of DEF is then $6 + \dfrac{x}{3} + \dfrac{x}{3} = 6 + \dfrac{2x}{3}$.

43. (D) $0.9(30) = 27$

44. (B) Since A is equilateral, one side of A has a length of $\dfrac{9}{3} = 3$. Using the ratio, with b representing the length of one side of triangle B, $\dfrac{3}{b} = \dfrac{6}{7}$, or $21 = 6b$. Therefore, $b = \dfrac{21}{6} = \dfrac{7}{2}$.

45. (D) The given equation can be rewritten as $5x = y$. Further, since the area of $ABPQ$ is $4x = 12$, we can find $x = 3$, which means $y = 5(3) = 15$. Therefore, the area of $ABCD$ is $4(3 + 15) = 4(18) = 72$.

46. (C) Because $\dfrac{x}{y} = \dfrac{2}{3}$, we can find $3x = 2y$ and $y = \dfrac{3}{2}x$. Given that $x + y = 125$, we can write $x + \dfrac{3}{2}x = \dfrac{5}{2}x = 125$, so $x = \dfrac{2}{5}(125) = 50$.

47. (B) Since the answer choices are given as fractions, express the percentage in fraction form: $\dfrac{0.2}{100}\left(\dfrac{1}{5}\right) = \dfrac{2}{1000}\left(\dfrac{1}{5}\right) = \dfrac{1}{500}\left(\dfrac{1}{5}\right) = \dfrac{1}{2500}$.

48. (C) The ratio $r : \pi r^2$ is equivalent to $1 : \pi r$.

49. (A) If P is the number of physics students and B is the number of biology students, then $3B = P$. Given $P = 21$, we can substitute and solve: $21 = 3B$, so $B = 7$.

50. (D) For some constant k, $m = \dfrac{k}{n}$. Given the initial values, $\dfrac{1}{2} = \dfrac{k}{6}$, so $k = 3$. When $n = \dfrac{2}{3}$, $m = \dfrac{3}{\left(\dfrac{2}{3}\right)} = 3\left(\dfrac{3}{2}\right) = \dfrac{9}{2}$.

51. (B) With the given information, we can write the equations $x = 0.3y$ and $0.2y = 8$. Solving the second equation, $y = 40$. Using this value of y in the first equation, $x = 0.3(40) = 12$.

52. (E) If y is directly proportional to x, then for some constant k, $y = kx$. Given the initial values, $6 = k\left(\dfrac{1}{4}\right)$ and $k = 24$. Therefore, $y = 24x$.

53. (E) Using the area of the rectangle, we can write $x(x + 1) = 12$, or $x^2 + x - 12 = 0$. Factoring, we see that $(x + 4)(x - 3) = 0$, and the equation has the solutions $x = -4$ and $x = 3$. Since the length must be positive, $x = 3$, and the ratio of x to $x + 1$ is 3 to 4.

54. (D) The length of one side of the square is $0.28(50) = 14$, so the area is $14 \times 14 = 196$.

55. (C) If $\dfrac{q}{100}(30) = 21$, then $q = 21\left(\dfrac{100}{30}\right) = 70$.

56. (C) After the first week, the price is $1.05(436) = 457.8$. After the second, the price is $0.9(457.8) = 412.02$, and after the third, $1.2(412.02) = 494.42$.

57. (D) The question describes $40\% + 10\% + 5\% = 55\%$ of the items, so the remaining items will be 45% of the total: $0.45(600) = 270$.

58. (C) The equation $a = 4\left(\dfrac{b}{2}\right)$ describes the relationship between a and b, and it can be simplified to $a = 2b$; solving for b, we have $b = \dfrac{1}{2}a$. Therefore, the percentage is

$$100\left(\frac{b}{a}\right)\% = 100\left(\frac{\frac{1}{2}a}{a}\right)\% = 50\%.$$

59. (E) To find the distance the particle will have moved in $2\dfrac{1}{4}$ hours, multiply the rate by the time: $\dfrac{3 \text{ units}}{\frac{1}{2}\text{ hr.}}\left(2\dfrac{1}{4}\text{ hr.}\right) = \dfrac{6 \text{ units}}{1 \text{ hr.}}\left(\dfrac{9}{4}\text{ hr.}\right) = 6\left(\dfrac{9}{4}\right)\text{ units} = \dfrac{27}{2}\text{ units}.$ It is moving along the x-axis from the origin, so the y-coordinate remains at zero, and in $2\dfrac{1}{4}$ hours it will arrive at the point with coordinates $x = \dfrac{27}{2}, y = 0$.

60. (B) Given the ratio, we can write $\dfrac{x}{y} = \dfrac{1}{4}$, or $4x = y$. Using the Pythagorean theorem, $x^2 + y^2 = (2\sqrt{17})^2$. Substituting the value for y from the first equation, $x^2 + (4x)^2 = 4(17)$, and $17x^2 = 68$. Finally, dividing both sides by 17 gives us $x^2 = 4$, and since x must be positive, $x = 2$.

61. (C) Because they lie on the same line, $m + n = 180$. Using the given ratio, $\dfrac{m}{n} = \dfrac{2}{3}$, so $3m = 2n$ and $m = \dfrac{2}{3}n$. Combining equations, $m + n = \dfrac{2}{3}n + n = \dfrac{5}{3}n = 180$, and $n = 180\left(\dfrac{3}{5}\right) = 108$.

62. (C) The second equation can be written as $3n = 4x$ or $n = \dfrac{4}{3}x$. Therefore, $\dfrac{m}{n} = \dfrac{4}{9} = \dfrac{m}{\left(\frac{4}{3}x\right)}$. Multiplying both sides by $\dfrac{4}{3}$ gives us $\dfrac{m}{x} = \left(\dfrac{4}{3}\right)\dfrac{4}{9} = \dfrac{16}{27}$.

63. (A) $\dfrac{1}{5}$ is half as large as $\dfrac{2}{5}$, and half of 10 is 5.

64. (A) $\dfrac{1 \text{ flash}}{6 \text{ min.}}(800 \text{ min.}) = 133.33$ flashes, or 133 complete flashes

65. (A) The length of AB is the height of ABC and ACE, so it is best to find it first. Since $AC = 4$ and $BC = 1$, by the Pythagorean theorem, $(AB)^2 + 1^2 = 4^2$ and $AB = \sqrt{15}$. Substitute this value of the height to find the areas of ACE and ABC: area of $ACE = \frac{1}{2}bh = \frac{1}{2}(2)(\sqrt{15}) = \sqrt{15}$; area of $ABC = \frac{1}{2}(1)(\sqrt{15}) = \frac{\sqrt{15}}{2}$. The ratio is therefore $1:\frac{1}{2}$, or 2:1.

66. (C) Simplify the expression for the information given: $\dfrac{\left(\dfrac{1}{2}\right)}{100}\left(\dfrac{x}{14}\right) = \dfrac{1}{200}\left(\dfrac{x}{14}\right) = \dfrac{x}{2800}$.

Next solve the given equation: $\dfrac{x}{2800} = \dfrac{1}{4}$, so $4x = 2800$ and $x = 700$.

67. (C) $1.03 \times 1.03 \times 1.03 \times \$675 = \$737.59$

68. (B) Cross multiply and solve for y: $14x = 4y$, and $y = \dfrac{14}{4}x = \dfrac{7}{2}x$.

69. (B) $100\left(\dfrac{45-38}{38}\right)\% = 18.4\%$

70. (D) In the first two hours of work, Harrison filed 28 folders. After that, he added 22 folders for each of the remaining (H − 2) hours. The function that models this is F = 28 + 22(H − 2).

Chapter 2

71. (B) First, the slanted distance of one side of the roof needs to be calculated from the Pythagorean formula: $\sqrt{25^2 + (18-10)^2} = 26.25$ ft. The perimeter of the house that requires trim (excluding the base) includes two slants and two side walls: $2*26.25 + 2*10 = 72.5$ ft. The trim around the square window and the top and sides of the door is: $4*4 + 2*6 + 3 = 31$ ft. The total trim is 72.5 ft + 31 ft = 103.5 ft. Multiplying this number by a cost of \$0.50 per foot, the total cost of the trim is \$51.75, which rounds to \$52.

72. (C) First, the area of the building needs to be calculated. The triangular part at the top of the house has a base of 50 feet and a height of 8 feet, and the area is calculated as $\frac{1}{2}(base)(height) = \frac{1}{2}(50)(8) = 200$ ft^2. The rest of the front of the house is a rectangle with an area of $base * height = 50*10 = 500$ ft^2. The area of the door and the window that do not need paint is $4*4 + 6*3 = 34$ ft^2. The total area that needs painting is 200 ft^2 + 500 ft^2 − 34 ft^2 = 666 ft^2. With two coats of paint this must be multiplied by two, giving a total area of 1332 ft^2. Dividing this value by 400 ft^2 of coverage for each gallon of paint gives 3.33 gallons. Therefore, 4 gallons must be purchased for the project.

73. (D) In quadrant I, the signs on x and y are positive, while in quadrant III, the signs on x and y are negative. In quadrant II, the sign on y is positive, while the sign on x is negative, and in quadrant IV, the sign on x is positive, while the sign on y is negative.

74. (B) Since the angle between the lines is 90 degrees, the lines are perpendicular, and the slopes are negative reciprocals of each other.

75. (A) Since the line rises from left to right, the slope is positive. However, the line crosses the x-axis to the right of the origin, so its x-intercept is positive. It crosses the y-axis below the origin, so its y-intercept is negative.

76. (E) Since the rectangles are similar and $3(5) = 15$, the length of the larger rectangle is $3(14) = 42$, and the perimeter is $15 + 42 + 15 + 42 = 114$.

77. (B) Since AB is a line, the sum of $5x$ and x must be 180 degrees. Thus, $5x + x = 6x = 180$, and $x = 180/6 = 30$.

78. (B) The sum of the measures of angles APD and APC must be 180 degrees, since DPC lies on the same line. Since the measure of APD is 80 degrees, angle APC must have a measure of $180 - 80 = 100$ degrees.

79. (C) Since the lines m and n are parallel, $y = 75$ (corresponding angles). And since the angles lie on the same line, $y + 3x = 180$. Therefore, $75 + 3x = 180$, and $x = 35$.

80. (C) The x-intercept for the line in answer choice C is 5, while the y-intercept is 2.

81. (D) By definition, the angle between two perpendicular lines is 90 degrees.

82. (D) If the radius is 2, then the lengths of line segments AP and PD are 2. Since AB is parallel to the x-axis, P has coordinates $(3, 4)$. Further, since DC is perpendicular to AB, the coordinates of D are $(3, 4 + 2)$, or $(3, 6)$.

83. (E) If $xy > 0$, then the individual values of x and y must have the same sign. Only points in the first and the third quadrants have the same sign.

84. (A) If both are positive, then the line will have to fall from left to right. If both are negative, the same is true.

85. (D) Any line with a slope of zero will be parallel to the x-axis.

86. (C) Sketching this triangle, you will see that it is a right triangle. The base is the line segment AC, and the height is the line segment AB. These line segments have lengths of 4 and 8, respectively. Using the formula for the area of a triangle, the area is thus $\frac{1}{2}(4)(8) = 16$ square units.

87. (E) For each of the given angles, the angle directly across from it will have the same measure. Moving up along line m, this gives the angles as z, x, and y. Since these angles are all along the same line, $x + y + z = 180$.

88. (D) To be along the circumference of the circle, the point must be exactly 2 units away from the point $(0, 7)$. Only the point $(1, 7)$ is not exactly 2 units from $(0, 7)$, as it is 1 unit away.

89. (B) A line with positive slope will rise from left to right, and a line with a negative x-intercept will cross the x-axis to the left of the origin.

90. (B) The y-intercept always occurs at the point where $x = 0$.

91. (D) Since the triangles are similar, $ED = 3y$, and the area is $\frac{1}{2}(3x)(3y) = \frac{9xy}{2}$.

92. (D) In the equation, let $y = -5$. This yields $-25 - 2x = -30$, or $-2x = -5$, which has a solution of $x = 5/2$.

93. (B) The angles discussed all lie along the same line. Therefore, if x is the measure of angle MQN, then $\frac{1}{2}x + x + \frac{1}{2}x = 180$, which simplifies to $2x = 180$, so $x = 90$. Therefore, the measure of PQM is 45 degrees, which is the same as the measure of angle NQR.

94. (A) The angle between any two perpendicular lines is 90 degrees. Therefore, we can write the equation $2x + 2 = 90$. Simplifying, $2x = 88$, which yields a solution of $x = 44$.

95. (C) The interior angles of any triangle must sum to 180. Therefore, the missing angle has a measure of $180 - 45 - 90 = 45$ degrees.

96. (C) The perimeter is the total distance around the rectangle. Here that distance is $4 + 10 + 4 + 10 = 28$.

97. (C) The sides of a square all have the same length, so if the area is 16, the length of any side, including the side AB, is 4. The line segment AB is also the radius of the circle, which is required to find the circumference. Using the formula, the circumference is $2\pi r = 8\pi$.

98. (A) The area of any circle is πr^2, where r is the radius. The radius of this circle is therefore $\sqrt{8} = 2\sqrt{2}$.

99. (C) Since two of the angles are equal, this must be an isosceles triangle. Since the two larger angles are equal, the two longer sides must be equal in measurement. Thus, the sides must have lengths 10, 20, and 20, giving a perimeter of 50.

100. (B) If the length of any one side of the square is x, then the area is x^2, and the perimeter is $4x$. If the area is twice the perimeter, $x^2 = 2(4x)$, and $x^2 - 8x = 0$. By factoring, we see this equation is equivalent to $x(x - 8) = 0$, which has solutions 0 and 8. The length cannot be 0, so it must be 8 units.

101. **(C)** To find the area of the rectangle, we need to know the length of the rectangle. The diagonal, the width, and the length form a right triangle. Further, since the hypotenuse of this triangle has a measure of 4(5) and one of the legs has a measure of 4(3), the triangle must be a 3-4-5 triangle, and the remaining leg has a measure of 4(4) = 16. Finally, the area of the rectangle will be 16 × 12 = 192.

102. **(D)** The smallest angle will correspond to one of the smallest sides, or to a side with length 3. Since the two smallest sides are equal, the triangle is isosceles, and there will be two angles with the given measure. Therefore, the remaining angle will have a measure of 180 − 30 − 30 = 120, confirming that it is the largest angle.

103. **(C)** Opposite angles in a parallelogram are congruent, so there are two angles of 50 degrees. Because a parallelogram is a quadrilateral, its interior angles sum to 360 degrees. Accounting for the two angles we already know, the remaining two angles must sum to $360 − 2(50) = 260$ degrees. Each of the larger angles therefore measures $\frac{260}{2} = 130$ degrees.

104. **(E)** The largest circle has a radius of 8 and therefore an area of 64π, while the inner circle has a radius of 2 and therefore an area of 4π. The area of the shaded region is the difference between these two areas: $64\pi − 4\pi = 60\pi$.

105. **(A)** The interior angles of any quadrilateral sum to 360 degrees. Therefore, $x = 360 − 125 − 75 − 105 = 55$.

106. **(B)** Given that the measure of CAB is 85 degrees, then the measure of ACB is as well, since $AB = BC$. Further, A, C, and D lie on the same line, so the angle BCD is $180 − 85 = 95$ degrees.

107. **(C)** The circumference is 6π, so for a radius r, $2\pi r = 6\pi$, and $r = 3$. The area is then $\pi(3^2) = 9\pi$.

108. **(D)** The volume of any cube is s^3, where s is the length of any one side. Here, $s^3 = 8$, so $s = 2$ (the cube root of 8). This means that $AB = AD = 2$, and by the Pythagorean theorem, $BD = \sqrt{2^2 + 2^2} = \sqrt{8} = 2\sqrt{2}$.

109. **(B)** The right triangle is a 45-45-90 triangle, and with such a triangle the two equal sides (which are across from the 45-degree angles) will always have the same value—we can call it s—while the hypotenuse will always be $\sqrt{2}$ times larger than the value of either of these sides, or $s\sqrt{2}$. Looking at the figure, since the value of the identical sides is 5, you know that x will be $\sqrt{2}$ times larger than that, or $5\sqrt{2}$.

110. **(B)** The volume of any sphere is $\frac{4}{3}\pi r^3$, where r is the radius. In this case, $\frac{4}{3}\pi r^3 = 36\pi$, and $r^3 = \frac{3}{4}(36) = 27$. Finally, r, the cube root of 27, is 3.

111. **(C)** ABC is an equilateral triangle, so each angle has a measure of 60 degrees. The angle with a measure of x degrees is the result of bisecting, or halving, this 60-degree angle, so $x = 30$.

112. **(D)** The diagonal forms a right triangle with the width and the length acting as legs. Using the Pythagorean theorem, the length of the triangle will be $\sqrt{25^2 - 15^2} = \sqrt{400} = 20$, and the area will be $20 \times 15 = 300$.

113. **(B)** Opposite sides of a parallelogram are congruent. Therefore, $AB = CD = 3$, and $BC = AD = 7$. The perimeter of $ABCD$ is then $3 + 3 + 7 + 7 = 20$.

114. **(D)** The total volume of the container is $8 \times 4 \times 3 = 96$ cubic feet, and the volume of the sand is $8 \times 4 \times 1 = 32$ cubic feet. This leaves $96 - 32 = 64$ cubic feet of the container unfilled.

115. **(B)** The overlap is shared by both of the squares and has an area of 2. Using the left square, the unshaded portion is said to be the same size. These two pieces make up the square, so it must have an area of 4.

116. **(E)** The total area of all the individual rectangles representing rooms will represent the total square footage of carpet needed. The largest rectangle has dimensions of 40 ft. × 30 ft. and an area of 1200 sq. ft. The smallest has dimensions 10 ft. × 20 ft. = 200 sq. ft. Finally, there is a square with dimensions of 20 ft. × 20 ft. and an area of 400 sq. ft. The resulting total is $1200 + 200 + 400 = 1800$ sq. ft.

117. **(B)** As an isosceles triangle, ABC will have two sides of the same length and two angles of the same measure. Here it must be that angle BAC is also 40 degrees, so angle ABC is $180 - 40 - 40 = 100$ degrees. The height BD will bisect this angle, meaning $a = 50$.

118. **(A)** Since the angles are the interior angles of a triangle, their sum is 180 degrees: $x + 2x + 3x = 6x = 180$, and $x = 180/6 = 30$.

119. **(B)** Using the circle centered at B, the radius is $\sqrt{49} = 7$. This is also the length of AB and BC. Since the circle centered at D has the same area, $CD = DE = 7$, and the length of AE is $4(7) = 28$.

120. **(E)** The sum of each pair must be $180 - 72 = 108$ degrees. This is true of every pair except the pair in answer choice E.

121. **(D)** If the width is w, then $l = 5w$, and the perimeter is $w + 5w + w + 5w = 12w$.

122. **(C)** The area is the total of the area of the two triangles and the rectangle $FBCE$: $\frac{1}{2}(2)(2) + 3(2) + \frac{1}{2}(2)(2) = 2 + 6 + 2 = 10$.

123. **(B)** Since opposite sides of a parallelogram are congruent, the perimeter is $8 + 2x = 20$. To solve for x, subtract 8 from both sides and then divide by 2: $x = \frac{12}{2} = 6$.

124. **(A)** The area is found with the formula lw, where l is the length and w is the width. Therefore, $45 = 9l$, and $l = \frac{45}{9} = 5$.

125. (B) The total area of the surface to be painted is $\frac{1}{2}(2)(2)+12(2)+\frac{1}{2}(2)(2)=28$. If each tube can cover four square feet, the artist will need $\frac{28}{4}=7$ tubes of paint.

126. (C) In the area formula for a circle, the radius is squared. Tripling the diameter of a circle means that the radius has also been tripled, and as the square of 3 is 9, choice C is the correct answer. Another way to prove this is to let $d=6$ in the first circle, determine A, and then determine the area of B using $d=18$.

127. (A) Using the formula for the volume of a sphere and the given volume, $\frac{4}{3}\pi r^3 = \frac{32}{3}\pi$, and $\frac{32}{3}=\frac{4}{3}(8)$, so $r=2$.

128. (A) The triangle has two sides of equal length, so it is isosceles, and the angles opposite these sides have the same measure. Since B and C lie along the same line as these angles, $x=y$, and $x-y=0$.

129. (D) If s is a single side of the cube, $s^3=125$, and $s=5$. Therefore, a single face would have an area of $5\times5=25$.

130. (A) Area $=\frac{1}{2}(\text{base})(\text{height})=\frac{1}{2}xy=\frac{xy}{2}$

131. (C) Since BD is a diagonal, ABD is exactly half of the rectangle, and the area of $ABCD=2(6)=12$ square meters.

132. (B) If s is one side of the square, then $s^2=49$, and $s=7$. Therefore, the perimeter is $4(7)=28$.

133. (E) The height of triangle PQR will equal the length of BA and allow us to find the area. Because the sides of an equilateral triangle are equal, we can determine that the height h is a leg of a right triangle with hypotenuse of 2 and a leg of 1. Using the Pythagorean theorem, $1^2+h^2=2^2$, so $h=\sqrt{3}$. The area is then $4\sqrt{3}$.

134. (C) The given triangle has two angles with the same measure, but one of its sides has a different value (x is not equal to y). The triangle is therefore an isosceles triangle and has two sides of length x. The perimeter is then $x+x+y=2x+y$.

135. (D) The perimeter can be written as $2x+2y=32$. To simplify and solve for y, divide both sides by 2: $x+y=16$. Given $x=3y$, substitute and solve: $3y+y=4y=16$, and $y=4$. Therefore, $x=16-4=12$.

136. (B) Since N is the midpoint of AC, AC has a length of $2(3)=6$. Using the area formula and the given area, $\frac{1}{2}(6)(AB)=12$, and $AB=4$.

137. (D) The diagonal AC bisects the angle at point C. You can attempt to determine the interior angles of the triangle ABC, but if you recall that the adjacent angles of a rhombus always sum to 180 degrees, then you can simply use the equation $x = 180 - 60 = 120$.

138. (C) As a circle has 360 degrees total, to find x you must divide this amount by 8: $x = \dfrac{360}{8} = 45$.

139. (C) Circumference $= 2\pi r = 2\pi\left(\dfrac{1}{\pi}\right) = 2$

140. (C) The sum of the interior angles of any quadrilateral is 360 degrees. Therefore, $x + 2x + x + 45 + x + 55 = 360$, and $5x + 100 = 360$. This equation has a solution of $x = 52$.

Chapter 3

141. (B) Using J to represent Juan's exam score, his missing score may be found as follows: $Average = \dfrac{Sum\ of\ all\ scores}{\#\ of\ scores}$. Plugging in what is known: $84 = \dfrac{76 + 88 + J + 75 + 92}{5}$. Cross multiplying: $84(5) = 76 + 88 + J + 75 + 92$. Solving this equation, $J = 89$. To find the median exam score, arrange the scores from lowest to highest and choose the middle student: Sarita (75), George (76), Tamara (88), Juan (89), Alesia (92). Tamara has the median score.

142. (D) The greatest common factor is the largest number that divides exactly into two or more numbers. With that in mind, this problem is best approached by elimination. Since each number ends in a zero, we know that each is divisible by 10. This means the correct answer must be either D or E. Checking, 130 is not divisible by 30, so the correct answer must be D.

143. (C) The list written in order from smallest to largest is 1, $\sqrt{2}$, $\sqrt{3}$, $\sqrt{5}$, 5. The median is the middle value of this list.

144. (E) Irrational numbers cannot be written as a fraction of two whole numbers. Each answer choice can be written as a whole number (which is the same as a fraction with a denominator of 1) or a fraction of whole numbers except answer choice E.

145. (B) The given information indicates that a is negative and both b and c are positive with b being larger than c. The difference $a - c$ (choice A) would be of the form (negative) − (positive), which is always negative. Since answer A states that $a - c > 0$ (is positive), choice A cannot be correct. The difference $c - b$ (choice B) will also always be negative, since b is larger than c. Unlike choice A, choice B states $c - b < 0$ (is negative), so this is the answer. The values of the remaining inequalities depend on the exact values of a, b, and c, which we do not know.

146. (C) The closest perfect square to 50 is $49 = 7 \times 7$. No integer larger than 7 is smaller than the square root of 50, since $8 \times 8 = 64$.

147. (A) $\dfrac{250}{10} = 25$

148. (A) An even number is defined as any number that can be written as a multiple of 2. Answer choice A is the only choice that can always be written as a multiple of 2 for any m and n, since it already is written in that form.

149. (E) Careful inspection of the answer choices shows that answer choice E is the same equation with the subtraction written differently. It is always true that $a - b = -b + a$. Since there can be only one correct answer, this must be it. However, the others can be shown to be incorrect by using different examples of x, y, and a.

150. (A) The correct answer will not be divisible by 7 but will be divisible by 2 and 3. This is the same as saying it is a multiple of 6 but not of 7. Answer choice A is equivalent to -9×6 and is not divisible by 7.

151. (C) The equation $\left| x - y \right| < \dfrac{1}{2}$ can be interpreted as "the distance between x and y is less than $\dfrac{1}{2}$." On the provided number line, only points C and D are less than one-half unit apart.

152. (A) $\dfrac{\left(\dfrac{5}{4} + \dfrac{1}{2} + \dfrac{x}{2} \right)}{3} = \dfrac{5}{12} + \dfrac{1}{6} + \dfrac{x}{6} = \dfrac{5}{12} + \dfrac{2}{12} + \dfrac{2x}{12} = \dfrac{2x+7}{12}$

153. (A) If $3(m + n)$ is even, then $m + n$ must be even, since the product of two odd numbers (that is, 3 and the sum of $m + n$) would be odd. It is possible that both m and n are even, but it is also possible that they are both odd. This eliminates the remaining answer choices.

154. (C) If a number is a multiple of both 4 and 9, then it is divisible by $4 \times 9 = 36$. All of the answer choices except C are divisible by 36.

155. (C) The 19 students in both bands are counted in both counts. Therefore, the total in only one band would be the sum of $(45 - 19)$ in performance band and $(30 - 19)$ in jazz band, which is $26 + 11$, or 37.

156. (E) The shaded region represents the set, and the open circle at 3 indicates it is not included in the set.

157. (D) The decimal forms of these numbers are easiest to rank from smallest to largest. Some of these values are easy to find or should have been memorized (as is true in the case of pi): $\left(\dfrac{1}{2} \right)^{-2} = 2^2 = 4$, $\dfrac{1}{3} = 0.\overline{3}$, $\pi \approx 3.14$. To estimate the square root values, consider perfect squares that are close in value: $\sqrt{3} < \sqrt{4} = 2$ and $\sqrt{3} > \sqrt{1} = 1$, and $4 = \sqrt{16} < \sqrt{17}$. The correct order is $\dfrac{1}{3}$, $\sqrt{3}$, π, $\left(\dfrac{1}{2} \right)^{-2}$, $\sqrt{17}$.

158. (E) It is possible that $pq = -2$, since $-2 \times -2 = 4$, so answer choices A and B can be eliminated. For answer choice C, it is possible that if the product of two numbers is 2 or -2, one of the numbers is a fraction. For example it could be that $p = \dfrac{1}{2}$ and $q = 4$. Similarly, for answer choice D, p and q could have the same sign or different signs, so this may or may not be true. Finally, in choice E, if p is larger than 2, then you would need to multiply it by something smaller to get a final product of 2. As an example, suppose that $p = 3$. Since $pq = 2$, then $q = \dfrac{2}{3}$. This makes answer choice E the only statement that would always be true.

159. (C) The median is the middle value when the numbers are placed in order. Since the number of values in the set is even, the middle will be the average of 2 and 4 (the two middle numbers), which is 3.

160. (D) $\left| -2(7) - 5 \right| - \left| -4 + 8 \right| = \left| -19 \right| - \left| 4 \right| = 19 - 4 = 15$

161. (B) Start by listing integers whose sum is 21: $1 + 20$, $2 + 19$, $3 + 18$, $4 + 17$, $5 + 16$, etc. The corresponding products keep increasing: 20, 38, 54, etc. Once you see that the products are increasing in this manner, the answer of 20 is the best choice.

162. (C) If $\dfrac{\sqrt{x}}{5}$ is an integer, then any integer multiple of it will also be an integer. Answer choice C is $\dfrac{1}{5} \times \dfrac{\sqrt{x}}{5}$, which may or may not be an integer, depending on the value of x.

163. (C) Factor out any perfect squares under both square roots: $\sqrt{48} - \sqrt{27} = \sqrt{3 \times 16} - \sqrt{3 \times 9} = 4\sqrt{3} - 3\sqrt{3} = \sqrt{3}$.

164. (C) The closest integer value to $\sqrt{26}$ is 5, since $\sqrt{25} = 5$. Similarly, $\sqrt{49} = 7$ is the integer closest to $\sqrt{50}$. Therefore, to satisfy the inequality, a value of x must be larger than 5 but no more than a little larger than 7 (and smaller than 8, since $8 \times 8 = 64$).

165. (A) $-2\left| -1 + 5 \right| = -2\left| 4 \right| = -2 \cdot 4 = -8$

166. (C) Rational numbers can be written as fractions of whole numbers. It is helpful to know some of the common irrational numbers; two of these are $\sqrt{2}$ and $\sqrt{3}$. Since answer choices A, B, D, and E contain these values, check the value of the remaining choice first: $\dfrac{\sqrt{100}}{5} = \dfrac{10}{5} = 2$.

167. (E) Note that y might be negative. If this is the case, it could still be that y^2 is larger than the positive number x, since the square of any negative number is positive. This eliminates answer choices A and B. Answer choices C and D will be true for some values but not for others, while answer choice E is always true, since x is already smaller than y^2.

168. (B) $\sqrt{-1 + (-(-1))^2} = \sqrt{-1 + 1^2} = \sqrt{-1 + 1} = \sqrt{0} = 0$

169. (B) The value of $\dfrac{\sqrt{26}}{5}$ will be a little larger than the value of $\dfrac{\sqrt{25}}{5} = \dfrac{5}{5} = 1$. In this case, the next positive integer will be the smallest integer that is larger. In this case, that is 2.

170. (A) Substituting values from the number line into the equation, the point A or $x = -4$ will satisfy the given inequality.

171. (B) The form of any odd integer is $2k + 1$ where k is any integer. The only answer choice with this form is answer choice B.

172. (D) If a number is in P, it is divisible by 5, and if a number is in Q, it is positive and less than 10. The only number that satisfies both properties is 5.

173. (B) Multiples of 12 include 12, 24, 48, 60, 72, 84, 96, 108, 120, 132, etc.; multiples of 20 include 20, 40, 60, 80, 100, 120, etc.; and multiples of 40 include 40, 80, 120, etc. The smallest multiple shared by all the given numbers is 120.

174. (E) It is possible that p is very close to 5 and q is very close to 4. This would make their product very close to 20. The smallest integer that would be greater would have to be 21.

175. (E) If a number has prime factors of 2, 3, and 7, it must be divisible by each of these values but by no other prime. In this case, $84 = 2^2 \cdot 3 \cdot 7$.

176. (C) Those signed up for two races are counted in both totals. Therefore, the total who signed up for only one race would be $53 - 12 + 21 - 12 = 50$.

177. (A) Another way to state the given information is that $x + 4$ must be a multiple of 4. Of the given possibilities, this is true only when $x = -16$.

178. (A) The inequality given is representing the set of numbers between -1 and 5, including the -1 but not including the 5. The set in answer choice A does not include the -1 and contains only negative numbers.

179. (B) If $x \rhd (-1) = \dfrac{-1}{x}$ is positive, x must be negative, since a negative number divided by a negative number is always positive.

180. (B) The number 100 can be factored as $10 \times 10 = 2 \times 5 \times 2 \times 5$. The numbers 2 and 5 are the distinct prime factors of 100, so $m = 2$ and $3m = 6$.

181. (D) $(6a^5)^2 = 6^2 a^{5 \times 2} = 36a^{10}$

182. (E) Given that the average of 12 numbers is m and if x represents the total of those numbers, then $\dfrac{x}{12} = m$ and $x = 12m$. Therefore, the average of these 12 numbers and 5 would be $\dfrac{12m + 5}{13}$.

183. (C) The value $|x - y|$ can be thought of as the number of units between x and y on a number line. In this case, x and y are more than 1 unit apart, so $|x - y| > 1$.

184. (B) The total is 650, and $147 + 335 + 98 = 580$ are already accounted for, so there must be $650 - 580 = 70$ remaining.

185. (C) Let the five numbers be represented by a, b, c, d, and e. Since the average of all five is 12.4, we know that $\dfrac{a+b+c+d+e}{5} = 12.4$, or $a+b+c+d+e = 12.4 \times 5 = 62$. We can say the four numbers that have an average of 11 are a, b, c, and d. This means that $\dfrac{a+b+c+d}{4} = 11$, or $a+b+c+d = 44$. Combining these equations, $(a+b+c+d)+e = 62 = 44+e$, so $e = 62 - 44 = 18$.

186. (B) Since the answer choices are written in terms of square roots, it is helpful to rewrite the given inequality in terms of square roots. Here, $\dfrac{3}{2} < x < \dfrac{5}{2}$ is equivalent to $\dfrac{\sqrt{9}}{2} < x < \dfrac{\sqrt{25}}{2}$. Of the answer choices, only $\dfrac{\sqrt{20}}{2}$ is between those values.

187. (A) The square of any number is always positive. Therefore, if xy^2 is negative, the value of x must be negative.

188. (E) When $x > 1$, $|x| = x$ and $\dfrac{|x|}{x} = \dfrac{x}{x} = 1$

189. (A) If the remainder of m divided by 2 is 1, then m must be odd. If m is odd, then $m + 1$ is even and a multiple of 2. Therefore, when $m + 1$ is divided by 2, there will be no remainder.

190. (A) If the median is 2, this means that when the numbers are placed in order from smallest to largest, 2 will be the middle number. Of the given answer choices, this only occurs when $x = 2$.

191. (A) $\left(\dfrac{1}{3}\right)^2 - \left(\dfrac{1}{2}\right)^{-1} = \dfrac{1}{9} - 2 = \dfrac{1}{9} - \dfrac{18}{9} = -\dfrac{17}{9}$

192. (C) Since the fraction is simplified, a cannot share any factors with 25 other than 1. The factors of 25 are 1, 5, and 25, and only answer choice C appears on this list.

193. (D) The expression $\dfrac{4^m}{4^n}$ is equivalent to the expression 4^{m-n}. For this expression to be smaller than 1, the exponent must be negative, so m must be smaller than n.

194. (A) Since we know that x is positive, the terms can be placed in order from smallest to largest: $-8x, -5x, -2x, x, 4x$. By definition, the median is the middle term in this list.

195. (A) The factors of $14a$ will include the factors of a (3 and 2), the factors of 14 (2 and 7), and all of their products. Of the answer choices, only 4 is a product of two of these factors (2 and 2).

196. (E) Let x represent the sum of the numbers. Then $\frac{x}{5} = 20$, and by cross multiplying, we see that $x = 100$.

197. (B) If x is the number in attendance on Friday, we can use the formula $\frac{32 + 34 + x}{3} = 32$

to find x. This formula is equivalent to $66 + x = 96$, which has a solution of $x = 30$.

198. (C) The smallest average that would allow for the salesperson to get a commission is \$250. Therefore, if x represents the person's sales on Friday, it must be that $\frac{98 + 255 + 175 + 320 + x}{5} = 250$, and $848 + x = 1250$. This equation has a solution of $x = 402$.

199. (C) Because the three-digit number has an odd number in the tens digit, there are 5 possible values for that digit. Further, the first digit can be any value 1–9, and the last digit can be any value 0–9. Using the multiplication rule, there are $9 \times 5 \times 10 = 450$ possibilities.

200. (D) If x is the total rain over the past six days and the average is 3.22, then $\frac{x}{6} = 3.22$, so

$x = 19.32$. For the average over seven days to be 3.40, it must be true that $\frac{19.32 + y}{7} = 3.4$,

where y is the rainfall on the seventh day. This equation has a solution of 4.48.

Chapter 4

201. (A) To organize the matrix equations, rearrange the equations so the variables are on the left in order of I_1, I_2, and I_3 with their respective coefficients and bring all the values without variables to the right-hand side: Equation 1: $I_1 + I_2 + I_3 = 0$. Equations: $10I_1 - 20I_2 + 0I_3 = -10$. Equation 3: $0I_1 + 20I_2 - 30I_3 = -30$. When the coefficients of each variable are organized in a 3×3 matrix, the following matrix is obtained:

$$\begin{bmatrix} 1 & 1 & 1 \\ 10 & -20 & 0 \\ 0 & 20 & -30 \end{bmatrix} \begin{bmatrix} I_1 \\ I_2 \\ I_3 \end{bmatrix} = \begin{bmatrix} 0 \\ -10 \\ -30 \end{bmatrix}$$

202. (C) Since $\vec{r} = \vec{s}$, then the corresponding cells of each vector are equal. The equation for the top cell is $2x = x - 4$ for which $x = -4$ is a solution. The equation for the bottom cells is $3y = 9$ for which $y = 3$ is a solution.

203. (A) $\dfrac{\sqrt{5}}{\sqrt{5}-1} = \dfrac{\sqrt{5}}{(\sqrt{5}-1)} \cdot \dfrac{(\sqrt{5}+1)}{(\sqrt{5}+1)} = \dfrac{\sqrt{5}\cdot\sqrt{5}+\sqrt{5}}{5-\sqrt{5}+\sqrt{5}-1} = \dfrac{5+\sqrt{5}}{4}$

204. (C) $xy = a^{3c}\cdot b^{2c} = (a^3)^c\cdot(b^2)^c = (a^3 b^2)^c$

205. (E) Recall that $i^2 = -1$. Multiplying the two complex numbers gives
$(4i - 4)\cdot(-2i + 4) = (4i)(-2i) + (4i)4 - 4(-2i) - 4(4) = -8i^2 + 16i + 8i - 16 = (-8)(-1) + 24i - 16 = 24i - 8$.

206. (D) $2.\overline{17} - 2.17 = 2.17171717\ldots - 2.17 = 0.00171717\ldots = 0.00\overline{17}$

207. (E) First, a common denominator must be found: $\dfrac{x-3}{x+5} + \dfrac{x}{5} = \dfrac{5(x-3)}{5(x+5)} + \dfrac{(x+5)x}{5(x+5)}$.
Now the numerators may be added and simplified: $\dfrac{5(x-3)+(x+5)x}{5(x+5)} = \dfrac{5x-15+x^2+5x}{5(x+5)} =$
$\dfrac{x^2+10x-15}{5(x+5)}$

208. (C) Two facts are important here: First, anything to the zero power is 1. Second, $\dfrac{1}{n} = a^{-n}$. Using these facts, the given equation becomes $1 = \dfrac{1}{(1-n)^3}$. The only way this fraction will be equivalent to 1 is if the denominator also is 1. Of the values given, the only value of n for which this is true is 0.

209. (D) $1 + \sqrt{-(-5)^2} = 1 + \sqrt{-25} = 1 + 5i$. The variable i represents the concept of an imaginary number, and in mathematical terms $i^2 = -1$.

210. (D) First simplify the expression on the left: $\left(2^{-\frac{1}{2}}\right)^{4y} = 2^{-2y} = \dfrac{1}{2^{2y}}$. It was given that this expression equals $\dfrac{1}{8}$, and $8 = 2^3$, so $2y = 3$ and $y = \dfrac{3}{2}$.

211. (E) For some value of k, $m = kn^2$. Using the given values to find k, $2 = k(-1)^2$ and $k = 2$. Therefore, $m = 2n^2$, and when $n = x+5$, $m = 2(x+5)^2 = 2(x^2+10x+25) = 2x^2 + 20x + 50$.

212. (D) Imaginary numbers are multiples of $i = \sqrt{-1}$. Answer choice D is $\sqrt{-49} = 7\sqrt{-1} = 7i$.

213. (D) The equation $m^{-3} = 64$ is equivalent to $\dfrac{1}{m^3} = 64$. To solve for m, cross multiply: $64m^3 = 1$. Collect terms and solve: $m^3 = \dfrac{1}{64}$, so $m = \dfrac{1}{4}$. The question asks for the value of $8m$: $8\left(\dfrac{1}{4}\right) = 2$.

214. (E) Exponents distribute over multiplication, and when an exponential term is taken to another exponent, you multiply the exponents to simplify the expression. Therefore, $(2m^3)^4 = 2^4 m^{3\times 4} = 16m^{12}$.

215. (A) When multiplying terms with exponents and the same base, add the exponents: $(10a^2)(5ab)(2ab^4) = 10\times 5\times 2\times a^{2+1+1}b^{1+4} = 100a^4b^5$.

216. (A) The imaginary number i represents $\sqrt{-1}$. Therefore, $i^2 = (\sqrt{-1})^2 = -1$.

217. (E) $M - 4N = \begin{bmatrix} 2 & -1 \\ 5 & 3 \end{bmatrix} - 4\begin{bmatrix} 1 & 0 \\ 0 & 1 \end{bmatrix} = \begin{bmatrix} 2 & -1 \\ 5 & 3 \end{bmatrix} - \begin{bmatrix} 4 & 0 \\ 0 & 4 \end{bmatrix} = \begin{bmatrix} (2-4) & -1 \\ 5 & (3-4) \end{bmatrix} =$

$\begin{bmatrix} -2 & -1 \\ 5 & -1 \end{bmatrix}$

218. (B) $6\begin{bmatrix} x \\ y \end{bmatrix} = 3\begin{bmatrix} 4 \\ 10 \end{bmatrix}$ may be rewritten as $\begin{bmatrix} 6x \\ 6y \end{bmatrix} = \begin{bmatrix} 3(4) \\ 3(10) \end{bmatrix}$ or $\begin{bmatrix} 6x \\ 6y \end{bmatrix} = \begin{bmatrix} 12 \\ 30 \end{bmatrix}$.

Setting the top terms equal $6x = 12$ thus $x = 2$. Setting the bottom terms equal $6y = 30$ thus $y = 5$. Finally, $y - x = 5 - 2 = 3$.

219. (D) The magnitude of a vector is found by applying the Pythagorean theorem to the two components of the vector $|\vec{r}| = \sqrt{4^{2+}(-3)^2} = 5$.

220. (D) The equation $2^{-m} = \dfrac{1}{8}$ is equivalent to $2^m = 8$. Since $8 = 2^3$, the value of m must be 3.

221. (B) $9(10) - 10^2 = 90 - 100 = -10$

222. (B) $\dfrac{(i-1)^2}{(i+1)^2} = \dfrac{i^2 - 2i + 1}{i^2 + 2i + 1} = \dfrac{-1 - 2i + 1}{-1 + 2i + 1} = \dfrac{-2i}{2i} = -1$

223. (B) The matrix equation may be rewritten as $\begin{bmatrix} 2b & -1b \\ 5b & 3b \end{bmatrix} = \begin{bmatrix} x & y \\ 5z & 9 \end{bmatrix}$. Cells (2, 2) are set equal to find the value of the real number b: $3b = 9$, so $b = 3$. Now cells (1, 1) are set equal to find the value for x: $2b = x$, so $x = 2(3) = 6$. Now cells (1, 2) are set equal to find the value for y: $-1b = y$, so $y = -1(3) = -3$. Now cells (2, 1) are set equal to find the value for z: $5b = 5z$, so $z = b = 3$. Finally, $x + y + z = 6 + (-3) + 3 = 6$.

224. (E) Recall that $a^{-n} = \dfrac{1}{a^n}$. Therefore, $\left(\dfrac{1}{4m^3} \right)^{-2} = (4m^3)^2 = 4^2 m^{3 \times 2} = 16m^6$.

225. (E) Given that a is a positive integer, $\left(\dfrac{1}{a} \right)^2 < \dfrac{1}{a}$, since the square is just the product of two fractions, so we can eliminate choice C. Similarly, $\dfrac{1}{a} < a < a^2$, which eliminates answer choices A and B. Considering answer choices D and E, $\left(\dfrac{2}{a} \right)^2 = 4 \left(\dfrac{1}{a} \right)^2$, so it is larger, and $\left(\dfrac{1}{2a} \right)^2 = \dfrac{1}{4} \left(\dfrac{1}{a} \right)^2$, so it is smaller.

226. (A) First, rationalize and simplify the two terms as follows: $\dfrac{3}{\sqrt{3}} + \dfrac{\sqrt{3}}{\sqrt{6}} = \dfrac{3 \, (\sqrt{3})}{\sqrt{3} \, (\sqrt{3})} + \dfrac{\sqrt{3} \, (\sqrt{6})}{\sqrt{6} \, (\sqrt{6})} = \dfrac{3\sqrt{3}}{3} + \dfrac{\sqrt{18}}{6} = \sqrt{3} + \dfrac{\sqrt{9(2)}}{6} = \sqrt{3} + \dfrac{3\sqrt{2}}{6} = \sqrt{3} + \dfrac{\sqrt{2}}{2}$. Finally, get a common denominator $= \dfrac{2\sqrt{3}}{2} + \dfrac{\sqrt{2}}{2} = \dfrac{\sqrt{2} + 2\sqrt{3}}{2}$.

227. (B) When $x = 1$, then $f(1) = 1^3 - 3(1) = -2$.

228. (B) $B - A = \begin{bmatrix} 3 & -2 \\ -8 & 5 \end{bmatrix} - \begin{bmatrix} 2 & -1 \\ 5 & 3 \end{bmatrix} = \begin{bmatrix} (3-2) & (-2+1) \\ (-8-5) & (5-3) \end{bmatrix} = \begin{bmatrix} 1 & -1 \\ -13 & 2 \end{bmatrix}$

229. (A) $\dfrac{i^5}{(i-1)} \times \dfrac{i^8}{(i+1)} = \dfrac{i(i^4)(i^2)^4}{i^2 - 1} = \dfrac{i(1)(1)}{-1 - 1} = -\dfrac{i}{2}$

230. (D) $\sqrt[3]{x^{12}} = (x^{12})^{\frac{1}{3}} = x^{\frac{12}{3}} = x^4$

231. (B) Since $16^{\frac{1}{2}} = \sqrt{16} = 4$, we are looking for a power of 2 that is less than 4 but larger than 0. Only the number 2 satisfies this property.

232. (E) The closest values for whole number powers of 2 are $2^5 = 32$ and $2^6 = 64$. Since 41 is between 32 and 64, m must be between 5 and 6.

233. (E) With $i^4 - i^6$, i^4 can be factored out so that the equations reads: $i^4(1 - i^2)$. Additionally, i^4 can be factored such that $(i^2)(i^2)$, so the equation could be written as: $(i^2)(i^2)(1 - i^2)$. Since the value of i^2 is given, substituting -1 for i^2 yields: $(-1)(-1)(1 - -1) = (1)(2) = 2$.

234. (D) $5\vec{r} - \vec{s} = 5\begin{bmatrix} 2 \\ 1 \end{bmatrix} - \begin{bmatrix} -2 \\ 0 \end{bmatrix} = \begin{bmatrix} 10 \\ 5 \end{bmatrix} + \begin{bmatrix} 2 \\ 0 \end{bmatrix} = \begin{bmatrix} 12 \\ 5 \end{bmatrix}$. The magnitude of this vector is found using the Pythagorean theorem: $|5\vec{r} - \vec{s}| = \sqrt{12^2 + 5^2} = 13$.

235. (B) For any values of p and q, $\dfrac{3^p}{3^q} = 3^{p-q}$. Therefore, because $81 = 3^4$, the difference of p and q must be 4.

236. (A) Substituting each of the values, $g(-4) = -6$.

237. (C) If $a^2 < a$, then a can be a positive fraction less than 1, and if $a^2 = a$, then a must be -1, 1, or 0. The values of a that satisfy the inequality $0 \le a \le 1$ would include some of these values and no others.

238. (A) $f(1) = 2(1)(1-1)^2 = 0$

239. (B) The value of any number taken to the zero power is 1.

240. (E) For some constant k, $y^2 = \dfrac{k}{x}$. Using the given values, $16 = \dfrac{k}{4}$ and $k = 64$. Therefore, when $x = 2$, $y^2 = \dfrac{64}{2} = 32$.

241. (C) $\dfrac{(2)^{\frac{20}{3}}}{(4)^{\frac{5}{2}}} = \dfrac{(2)^{\frac{20}{3}}}{(2^2)^{\frac{5}{2}}} = \dfrac{(2)^{\frac{20}{3}}}{(2)^5} = (2)^{\frac{20}{3}} \cdot (2)^{-5} = (2)^{\left(\frac{20}{3} - 5\right)} = (2)^{\left(\frac{20}{3} - \frac{15}{3}\right)} = (2)^{\left(\frac{5}{3}\right)} = \sqrt[3]{2^5}$

242. (E) For some constant k, $y = \dfrac{k}{\sqrt{x}}$. Using the given values, $18 = \dfrac{k}{\sqrt{4}}$ and $k = 36$. Therefore, when $x = 12$, $y = \dfrac{36}{\sqrt{12}} = \dfrac{36}{2\sqrt{3}} = \dfrac{18}{\sqrt{3}} = \dfrac{18\sqrt{3}}{3} = 6\sqrt{3}$.

243. (C) If $x^2 + 1 = 0$, then $x^2 = -1$ and $x = \pm\sqrt{-1} = \pm i$.

244. (D) $xy^4 + x^3 y = (4)(-1)^4 + 4^3(-1) = 4 - 64 = -60$

245. (D) $(-(-2))^2 - (-(-2)) = 2^2 - 2 = 4 - 2 = 2$

246. (D) Using the FOIL method, $(2m - 6)^2 = 4m^2 - 12m - 12m + 36 = 4m^2 - 24m + 36$.

247. (A) $f\left(\dfrac{1}{2}\right) = \dfrac{\left(\dfrac{1}{2}\right)^3}{4} = \dfrac{\left(\dfrac{1}{8}\right)}{4} = \dfrac{1}{32}$

248. (A) When a number is in front of a matrix, simply multiply each term in the matrix by that number: $-2\begin{bmatrix} 5 & -2 & 3 \\ 0 & 10 & -5 \end{bmatrix} = \begin{bmatrix} -2(5) & -2(-2) & -2(3) \\ -2(0) & -2(10) & -2(-5) \end{bmatrix} = \begin{bmatrix} -10 & 4 & -6 \\ 0 & -20 & 10 \end{bmatrix}$

249. (C) Remember that exponents must distribute to everything within the product.
Therefore: $\left(\dfrac{1}{2}x^2 y\right)^5 = \left(\dfrac{1}{2}\right)^5 x^{2\times5} y^{1\times5} = \dfrac{1}{2^5}x^{10}y^5 = \dfrac{1}{32}x^{10}y^5$.

250. (D) $\dfrac{i^4 - 5}{i^2} = \dfrac{(i^2)^2 - 5}{-1} = \dfrac{(-1)^2 - 5}{-1} = \dfrac{1 - 5}{-1} = \dfrac{-4}{-1} = 4$

Chapter 5

251. (C) The owner's fixed daily cost is $160 + \$200 = \$360$. The ingredients cost $2 per pizza, giving the total daily expenditure of $360 + 2n$. Divide this function by the number of pizzas (n) to get the cost per pizza: $\dfrac{360 + 2n}{n}$.

252. (D) When daily expenditure equals the daily gross income, the owner will "break even" and begin making a profit. As explained in the previous answer, the daily expenditures in terms of number of pizzas is $360 + 2n$. Since the average selling price per pizza is $14, the gross income after selling n pizzas during the day is $14n$. The following equation will determine the number of pizzas that need to be sold before a profit is made: $14n = 360 + 2n$. Isolating n: $12n = 360$. Dividing by 12, $n = 30$.

253. (E) The quadratic function $x^2 - 3x - 10$ factors into $(x - 5)(x + 2)$. This can equal zero only if $x = 5$ or $x = -2$.

254. (D) Cross multiplying will provide us with a linear equation to solve: $3m = 4(m - 1)$. To solve, distribute the 4 on the right side to get $3m = 4m - 4$, and then subtract $4m$ from both sides: $-m = -4$. If $-m = -4$, then $m = 4$.

255. (A) This is a system of equations. Adding the two equations gives the equation of one variable, $2x = -4$, which has a solution of $x = -2$. By substituting this value of x into the first equation, we find $-2 - y = -5$ and $y = 3$. Given these two values, we can calculate $xy = -2 \times 3 = -6$.

256. **(C)** Use the process of matrix multiplication: $\begin{bmatrix} -1 & 2 \\ 4 & 8 \end{bmatrix} \begin{bmatrix} 6 & 3 \\ 7 & -6 \end{bmatrix} =$

$$\begin{bmatrix} -1(6)+2(7) & -1(3)+2(-6) \\ 4(6)+8(7) & 4(3)+8(-6) \end{bmatrix} = \begin{bmatrix} 8 & -15 \\ 80 & -36 \end{bmatrix}.$$

257. **(E)** A root of a function is a solution to the equation formed when setting the function equal to zero. In this case, it would be a solution to $-5x + x^2 = 0$, which is equivalent to $x(-5 + x) = 0$ when x is factored out. Finally, by the zero product rule, the roots are $x = 0$ and $x = 5$.

258. **(E)** By factoring the given inequality, we see that it can be rewritten as $(m-5)(m-3) < 0$ and that the function has roots of 3 and 5. This means the function will be negative either before 3 ($m < 3$), after 5 ($m > 5$), or in between ($3 < m < 5$). By testing values, we can determine which is true. For values before 3, testing $m = 0$ yields $0^2 - 8(0) + 15 = 15 > 0$. For values after 5, $m = 6$ yields $6^2 - 8(6) + 15 = 3 > 0$. Finally, for values between 3 and 5, $m = 4$ yields $4^2 - 8(4) + 15 = -1 < 0$, showing us that the function is negative for all of these values.

259. **(C)** If we let the first integer be represented by x, then the second integer will be $x + 2$, since they are both odd. Therefore, $x + x + 2 = 256$, which simplifies to $2x + 2 = 256$, and $x = 127$. However, this is the value of the smaller of the pair; the larger is $x + 2 = 129$.

260. **(C)** Rewriting the first inequality shows that $2p + q > 5p$. Collecting terms, $q > 3p$. Therefore, when $p > 2$, $q > 6$.

261. **(E)** The terms in the numerator all have the same variable and the same degree, so they are like terms and can be added across: $\dfrac{x^2 - 4x^2 + x^2}{x} = \dfrac{-2x^2}{x}$. Since the numerator and the denominator share a factor of x, this is equivalent to $-2x$.

262. **(E)** Using the FOIL method, $(a-6)(b+4) = ab + 4a - 6b - 24$.

263. **(D)** For a system of equations to have infinite solutions, one of the equations must be a multiple of the other. Looking at the constant on the right side, the first equation would have to be multiplied by -3 to get from 2 to -6. Therefore, $m = -3(-3) = 9$, and $n = 1(-3) = -3$.

264. **(B)** For the inequality to be true, $\dfrac{x}{4}$ must be more than $\dfrac{1}{4}$ larger than 1 or simply equal to $1 + \dfrac{1}{4}$. Since $\dfrac{4}{4} = 1$, $\dfrac{4}{4} + \dfrac{1}{4} = \dfrac{5}{4}$ will satisfy the greater than or equal to condition, so $x = 5$.

265. (E) Notice that the expression on the right side of each answer choice is always $3x + 2y$. The only way to clear fractions in this way would be for us to multiply both sides of the equation by 6, which will yield the expression in answer choice E.

266. (A) Solving inequalities works the same way as solving equations. However, we must remember that multiplying or dividing both sides by a negative value will switch the order of the inequality. Therefore, when we simplify the inequality to $-3x > 2$, the solution becomes $x < -\dfrac{2}{3}$.

267. (D) Solving for a in both inequalities gives us $a \geq c + x$ and $a > c + x$. The only difference between these is that $a \geq c + x$ allows for a to equal $c + x$, while $a > c + x$ does not.

268. (B) If $3^{xy} = \dfrac{1}{9}$, then xy must be -2. Also, since $2x + y = 0$, $y = -2x$. Substituting this value of y into $xy = -2$ gives us $x(-2x) = -2$ or $-2x^2 = -2$, which has a solution of $x = 1$ or -1, but since the equation states that x is positive, the possibility that $x = -1$ may be discarded. If $x = 1$, then using the first equation, $y = -2$, and $x + y = 1 + (-2) = 1 - 2 = -1$.

269. (C) When $k = -1$, $\left(\dfrac{x+y}{k}\right)^2 = (-1)^2(x+y)^2 = (x+y)^2$. This expression can be simplified to $x^2 + 2xy + y^2$ by using the FOIL technique.

270. (D) In general, $\log_b x = a$ is equivalent to $b^a = x$. Here, $\log_2 x = 3$ implies $x = 2^3 = 8$.

271. (B) Using the FOIL method, $(x - a)(x + a) = x^2 + ax - ax - a^2 = x^2 - a^2$.

272. (A) We can factor x out of the equation $3x^2 - \dfrac{1}{2}x = 0$ to get the equivalent equation $x\left(3x - \dfrac{1}{2}\right) = 0$. Since this is the product of two terms, we can then apply the zero product rule to find $x = 0$ or $3x - \dfrac{1}{2} = 0$. The second equation has a solution of $x = \dfrac{1}{6}$.

273. (B) If, when added, the given equations result in an untrue statement, then the system will have no solutions. The coefficient of x in the second equation is 1, and it is 2 in the first equation. Therefore, if we make b half of 8 and c not equal to half of 2, we will end up with an untrue statement. The choice with this format is $b = 4$ and $c = 3$.

274. (B) To get $3m - 8$ from the given $3m - 4$, we must subtract 4 from both sides of the equation. On the right side, $6n - 8 - 4 = 6n - 12$.

275. (D) Substituting the given expression for a, we get $2\left(\dfrac{x}{y}\right) - \left(\dfrac{x}{y}\right)^2 = \dfrac{2x}{y} - \dfrac{x^2}{y^2}$. To simplify, we must find a common denominator. The common denominator is y^2, and the resulting expression is $\dfrac{2x}{y} - \dfrac{x^2}{y^2} = \dfrac{2xy}{y^2} - \dfrac{x^2}{y^2} = \dfrac{2xy - x^2}{y^2}$.

276. (C) Subtraction of matrices is performed by subtracting the corresponding entries. Therefore, $z = 4 - 1 = 3$.

277. (A) Each term in the numerator has a factor of 2. Factoring out this 2 results in the expression $\dfrac{2(3x - 2)}{2} = 3x - 2$.

278. (D) A good first step here is to divide both sides by 4. This simplifies the equation to $x - 1 = 2(x - 2)$, or $x - 1 = 2x - 4$. To solve, subtract x from both sides and then add 4, resulting in $x = 3$.

279. (E) The given inequality is equivalent to the inequality $\dfrac{5}{7} \leq x$, and every positive integer is larger than $\dfrac{5}{7}$.

280. (B) The sum of the expressions is $3x + 4x - 1 - 2x = 5x - 1$. Given that this sum is equal to 9, we can write the equation $5x - 1 = 9$ to find the value of x. Adding 1 to both sides, we find $5x = 10$ and $x = 2$.

281. (A) Begin by simplifying the equation using a like denominator: $\dfrac{1}{2a} + \dfrac{1}{a} = \dfrac{1}{2a} + \dfrac{2}{2a} = \dfrac{3}{2a} = 14$. Cross multiplying yields the equation $28a = 3$, so $a = \dfrac{3}{28}$.

282. (C) If x represents the size of his original collection, then the statements give us the equation $x + 36 = 2x$. Therefore, $x = 36$, and his current collection has a size of $36 + 36 = 72$.

283. (E) To solve for x, divide each term in the inequality by 5, and rewrite it as $-\dfrac{1}{10} \leq x \leq \dfrac{33}{10}$. Each value given is a solution to this inequality except 4, which is larger than $\dfrac{33}{10}$.

284. (D) If the smallest integer is x, then the next is $x + 1$, and the third is $x + 2$. The sum of these expressions is $3x + 3$.

285. (D) Factoring out a 5 from the given expression leaves us with $5\left(x - \dfrac{3}{2}\right)$, since $15 = 3 \times 5$.

286. (A) Adding the two equations, $3a = 6$, so $a = 2$. Substituting this into the first equation gives $2 - b = 7$, so $b = -5$.

287. (A) If x represents the amount of Type 1 in stock while y represents the amount of Type 2 in stock, $x = 2y$, and $x + y = 21{,}000$. If you plug the value of x ($x = 2y$) from the first equation into the second equation, you get $3y = 21{,}000$. Simplifying this yields $y = 7000$.

288. (B) Being careful to distribute the 2, this equation is equivalent to $6a - 1 = 2a + 2$. Simplifying, $4a = 3$, so $a = \dfrac{3}{4}$.

289. (C) After rewriting the equation as $3x^2 - 19x - 14 = 0$, we see that it factors into $(3x + 2)$ and $(x - 7)$. Therefore, the only positive solution will be $x = 7$.

290. (D) $6(m^2 n^2 - 1) = 6((mn)^2 - 1) = 6(4^2 - 1) = 6(16 - 1) = 6(15) = 90$

291. (D) Since the terms are not like terms, they cannot be combined at all, and answer choices A and B can be eliminated. In answer choices C and D, the term $-b$ has been factored out of $2b^2 + b$, and only answer choice D does so correctly. Answer choice E tries to factor out $2b$, but 2 is not a factor of b.

292. (E) $(2y - 1)^{-x} = (2y - 1)^{-\frac{1}{2}} = \dfrac{1}{(2y-1)^{\frac{1}{2}}} = \dfrac{1}{\sqrt{2y-1}}$

293. (B) Each inequality in the answer choices has the reverse direction of the one given. This must mean both sides were multiplied by -1. When both sides are multiplied by -1, the signs on every term will change.

294. (D) Since the term on the right side of the equation has a lower degree than the first term on the left side of the equation, the operation must have been division.

295. (A) Let x and y represent the two numbers. Here we can write $xy = 20$, and $x + y = 12$, so $y = 12 - x$. Substituting this expression for y into the first equation, we find that $x(12 - x) = 20$, which can be expressed as $x^2 - 12x + 20 = 0$. This equation factors into $(x - 2)(x - 10) = 0$, which has solutions 2 and 10. Finally, the difference is $10 - 2 = 8$.

296. (C) Subtracting x from both sides of the inequality yields $-y > y$. This can be true only when $y < 0$.

297. (E) The equation $\log_3(x - 1) = 2$ is equivalent to $x - 1 = 3^2$, which has a solution of $x = 9 + 1 = 10$.

298. (A) The roots of an expression are the solutions to that expression set equal to zero. Since this expression factors, the roots can be found by solving $(x - 2)(x - 1) = 0$. Of the roots 2 and 1, neither is larger than 5.

299. (A) Subtracting 5 from both sides of the inequality yields the inequality $-\dfrac{1}{2}x \geq 4$. To solve, multiply both sides by -2: $x \leq -8$.

300. (B) Multiplying the first equation by 2 and then adding equations results in the equation $7x = -14$, which has a solution of $x = -2$.

301. (B) The given log expression is equivalent to $x^4 = 16$. Since $16 = 4 \times 4 = 2 \times 2 \times 2 \times 2$, $x^4 = 2^4$, $x = 2$.

302. (D) To rationalize the denominator, we multiply the expression by $\dfrac{\sqrt{m}}{\sqrt{m}}$, so $\dfrac{m}{\sqrt{m}}\left(\dfrac{\sqrt{m}}{\sqrt{m}}\right)=\dfrac{m\sqrt{m}}{m}=\sqrt{m}$.

303. (C) If the product of a and $(a-1)$ is 6, then $a^2-a=6$, and $a^2-a-6=0$. This equation factors into $(a-3)(a+2)$, which has roots 3 and -2.

304. (E) To find the square of x, you must use the FOIL technique: $x^2=(k^2-2)^2=k^4-4k^2+4$.

305. (A) $(3x^2-5x+1)-(3x^2-2x+6)=3x^2-5x+1-3x^2+2x-6=-3x-5$

306. (B) The greatest common factor can be thought of as the "largest" term that will divide both terms. In this case, a^3 is the largest term that can divide both terms.

307. (C) Subtracting $\sqrt{y}$ from both sides simplifies the equation to $8=2\sqrt{y}$. Divide both sides by 2 to get $4=\sqrt{y}$. Squaring both sides of the equation then yields $y=16$.

308. (C) On the right side of the equation, both coefficients have been reduced by a factor of 5. Additionally, the power on n was reduced by 1 on each term. Therefore, $5n$ must have been the term factored out.

309. (C) Adding x and 5 to both sides of the equation yields $2x=14$, so $x=7$.

310. (E) All of the answer choices include the term $p+5$. The given inequality can be rewritten in terms of $p+5$ by adding 10 to both sides. The resulting inequality is $p+5>8$.

311. (D) The equation given is equivalent to $-k^2-k=0$, factored to $-k(k+1)=0$, which has roots of 0 and -1.

312. (C) $\dfrac{1-x^2}{x}=\dfrac{1}{x}-\dfrac{x^2}{x}=\dfrac{1}{x}-x$

313. (D) Each person will receive $\dfrac{m}{6}$ dollars. Therefore, two people together will receive $\dfrac{m}{6}+\dfrac{m}{6}=\dfrac{2m}{6}=\dfrac{m}{3}$ dollars.

314. (D) Substituting the value of y^2 from the second equation into the first, $2x+3x=7$, which simplifies to $5x=7$. To find $10x$, we multiply both sides of this equation by 2.

315. (C) $\dfrac{2x}{9}\times\dfrac{3}{x}=\dfrac{6x}{9x}=\dfrac{2}{3}$

316. (A) Since x is positive, only $-2x$ will be negative, and a negative number is always smaller than a positive number.

317. (B) When $y = 0$, $2x + 2 = -2$, which simplifies to $2x = -4$. This equation has a solution of $x = -2$.

318. (D) Multiples of $8a$ include $16a$, $24a$, $32a$, etc. Multiples of $6a$ include $12a$, $18a$, $24a$, etc. The smallest multiple shared on these two lists is $24a$.

319. (C) If the sum of n and 4 is 10, then we can write $n + 4 = 10$. Subtracting 5 from both sides, we find $n - 1 = 5$.

320. (E) The first inequality is equivalent to $x > \dfrac{3}{4}$, while the second is equivalent to $x < -3$.

There are no real numbers that are larger than $\dfrac{3}{4}$ and at the same time smaller than -3.

Chapter 6

321. (A) Since Mario's beginning mile marker (299) is greater than Kiyomi's mile marker (203) and he is moving south toward Kiyomi, his mile marker will decrease by 50 miles each hour. His mile marker is written as a function of elapsed time as follows: $M = -50t + 299$.

322. (A) To find the elapsed time when they reach the same position, the mile marker functions for both drivers are set equal to each other: $-50t + 299 = 70t + 203$. Isolating t, $96 = 120t$. Dividing by 120, $t = 0.80$ hr. $0.80 \text{ hr} \left(\dfrac{60 \text{ min}}{1 \text{ hr}} \right) = 48 \text{ min}$.

323. (D) In order to determine the binomials that make up this trinomial, you must experiment with some values. Since the middle value x has a -1 in front of it, it helps to work with two factors of -12 that might add up to -1 when combined. The numbers -4 and 3 fit this description, $x^2 - x - 12 = (x - 4)(x + 3)$.

324. (D) $(-2)\,\Xi\,(-3) = (-3)^2 - (-2)^2 + 1 = 9 - 4 + 1 = 6$

325. (B) The graph of $g(x)$ is a line, while the graph of $f(x)$ is a parabola (both ends either rising or falling). Therefore, the graphs of the functions may intersect 0, 1, or 2 times, meaning 2 is the maximum number of times.

326. (A) If $f(x)$ is a polynomial with the given zeros, then $(x + 3)$, $(x + 2)$, $(x - 4)$, $(x - 5)$, and $(x - 7)$ are factors of $f(x)$.

327. (D) A shift of $f(x)$ to the left c units is always represented by $f(x + c)$.

328. (B) We are given the y value and must find the x value. Substituting the given value into the function, $4 = 3q - 5$, and $9 = 3q$. Therefore, $q = 3$.

329. (C) $V(8) = 1000(1 + 0.06)^8 = 1593.85$

330. (E) The graph of x^2 crosses the x-axis at the origin, so choice A is not correct. Since this graph is centered along the y-axis, it must be a vertical translation of x^2. Further, since it has a positive y-intercept, it must be of the form $x^2 + c$, where c is positive, as in choice E.

331. (E) The graph of $-f(x)$ will be a reflection of the graph of $f(x)$.

332. (D) $f(a-1) = (a-1)^2 + (a-1) - 1 = a^2 - 2a + 1 + a - 1 - 1 = a^2 - a - 1$

333. (A) $-2 \ \nabla \ 1 = 2(-2) - 3(1) = -4 - 3 = -7$

334. (D) $(f \circ g)(3) = f(g(3)) = f(3^2 - 2) = f(7) = 7 + 6 = 13$

335. (B) To find the x value of the point where the graphs intersect, we set the expressions equal to each other and solve for x. Given that $64x^3 = 8$, we see that $x^3 = \dfrac{8}{64} = \dfrac{1}{8}$ and $x = \dfrac{1}{2}$.

336. (C) $g(\sqrt{3}) = (\sqrt{3})^4 + (\sqrt{3})^2 = 9 + 3 = 12$

337. (A) Factoring gives $x^2 + 2x - 35 = (x+7)(x-5) = 0$. By the zero product rule, $x + 7 = 0$ and $x - 5 = 0$. Therefore, the roots are -7 and 5. The question asks for the largest value, which is 5.

338. (A) Since the function is a polynomial that does not cross the x-axis at any other point, it will be of the form $(x + a)(x + b)(x - c)$ for positive a, b, and c, since the x-coordinates of A and B are negative while the x-coordinate of C is positive. Only choice A meets this condition.

339. (E) Dividing both sides of the equation by 2 gives an equivalent equation, $x^2 - 3x = -2$, which can be restated as $x^2 - 3x + 2 = 0$. Factor the equation to get $(x - 2)(x - 1) = 0$. By the zero product rule, $x = 2$ and $x = 1$. Therefore, there is no value $x < 0$ that makes the equation true.

340. (D) The expression $x^4 - 16$ is a difference of squares, so it factors into $(x^2 + 4)(x^2 - 4)$, which factors further into $(x^2 + 4)(x + 2)(x - 2)$.

341. (A) Given the table, $f(x) = 0$ when $x = -6$.

342. (E) The function $f(x) = 3x^2 - 3x - 27 = 0$ is equivalent to $\dfrac{1}{3}(3x^2 - 3x - 27) = \dfrac{1}{3}(0)$, or $x^2 - x - 9 = 0$.

343. (B) The 3 is added to the x before the term is squared, so the first two steps are $(x + 3)^2$. In the next step, this term is multiplied by 5.

344. (A) $f(2, -3) = 2(-3) - 2 = -6 - 2 = -8$

345. (C) Given that $-f(x) = -x^3$, then for $x = -2$, we find $-f(-2) = -(-2)^3 = -(-8) = 8$. For $x = -1$, we find $-f(-1) = -(-1)^3 = -(-1) = 1$. For $x = 0$, the solution is $-f(0) = -(0)^3 = 0$. For $x = 1$, it is $-f(1) = -(1)^3 = -(1) = -1$, and for $x = 2$, it is $-f(2) = -(2)^3 = -8$.

346. (E) The graph of $f(x - 2)$ would be the graph of $f(x)$ shifted to the right by 2 units. Therefore, every x-coordinate would be increased by 2.

347. (A) $7\Delta(-2) = \dfrac{7+1}{-2} = \dfrac{8}{-2} = -4$

348. (C) If $f(2) = 2$, then $\dfrac{-1}{k} = 2$ and $2k = -1$. Therefore, $k = -\dfrac{1}{2}$.

349. (A) If $x^2 = 72 - x$, then $x^2 + x - 72 = 0$. Factoring, $(x + 9)(x - 8) = 0$, and by the zero product rule, $x = -9$ and $x = 8$. The question asks for the smaller of these values.

350. (A) The resulting graph would be a parabola, which could be completely within the first quadrant.

351. (E) The graph of $g(x)$ will be reflected over the x-axis. Further, if $g(3) = 3$, then $-g(3) = -3$.

352. (E) The equation $2x^2 - 5x + 3 = x^2 - 5x + 2$ is equivalent to the equation $x^2 + 1 = 0$. This equation is equivalent to $x^2 = -1$, which has no real solutions.

353. (D) After $f(x)$ crosses the x-axis, it stays above it. Therefore, the function is positive for every x value after -4.

354. (B) $f(5) = \dfrac{5 - 4}{5 + 1} = \dfrac{1}{6}$

355. (C) $P(6) - P(5) = [8(6) - 5] - [8(5) - 5] = 43 - 35 = 8$

356. (D) We are given the x value and must find the corresponding y value. Given the expression for the function, $c = g(4) = \dfrac{3(4) + 10}{8} = \dfrac{22}{8} = \dfrac{11}{4}$.

357. (E) By the zero product rule, if the function is $(x - k)(f(x))$, then $x - k = 0$ and $f(x) = 0$ can be used to find the zeros of the function. Using the first equation, $x = k$ must be a zero of the function.

358. (B) The equation $f(g(x)) = 8$ is equivalent to $\dfrac{1}{2}(2x)^2 = 8$, or $\dfrac{1}{2}(4x^2) = 8$. Dividing both sides by 2, $x^2 = 4$ so $x = \pm\sqrt{4} = \pm 2$.

359. (E) In general, if a function $f(x)$ is shifted up by 6 units, the graph will be described by $f(x) + 6$. If that same graph is shifted to the left one unit, then the graph will be represented by $f(x + 1) + 6$. Applying this to the given expression, $(x - 5 + 1)^3 + 6 = (x - 4)^3 + 6$.

360. (D) The graph will be a downward-facing parabola with a line of symmetry through the x-axis. Since c is positive, $f(x) > 0$ when x is between -3 and 3 and $f(x) < 0$ otherwise. Finally, because of the symmetry, $f(-c) = f(c)$.

361. (C) For $a = 1$, substitute and simplify: $g(1, b) = 4b - b + 1 = 3b + 1 > 0$. For the inequality where $g(1, b) > 0$, solve for b: $3b + 1 > 0$, so $b > -\dfrac{1}{3}$.

362. (D) $(f \circ g)(7) = f(g(7)) = f(-5(7) - 8) = f(-43) = -43 + 10 = -33$

363. (B) The function $g(x)$ is greater than $f(x)$ whenever the graph of $g(x)$ is above the graph of $f(x)$. This occurs between the x values of -1 and 4.

364. (B) At some point in solving the given equation, the equation $x = -\dfrac{5}{2}$ must have been found. Work backward by adding $\dfrac{5}{2}$ to both sides and multiplying both sides by 2: $x + \dfrac{5}{2} = 0$, and $2x + 5 = 0$.

365. (E) $\dfrac{x^2 - 3x - 4}{x - 4} = \dfrac{(x - 4)(x + 1)}{x - 4} = x + 1, \ x \neq 4$

366. (C) To touch the x-axis at only one point and be a quadratic function as shown in the answer choices, the function would have to be of the form $(x + c)^2 = x^2 + 2xc + c^2$ or $(x - c)^2 = x^2 - 2xc + c^2$ for some value of c. The function in answer choice (C) is of this form, since $8 = 2(4)$ and $4^2 = 16$.

367. (E) $g(a^2 - 10) = (a^2 - 10)^2 + (a^2 - 10) - 5 = a^4 - 20a^2 + 100 + a^2 - 10 - 5 = a^4 - 19a^2 + 85$

368. (B) Since $x - 5$ is a factor, 5 must be a zero of the function, and $(5, 0)$ is on its graph.

369. (B) If $a < 0$, the graph is facing downward, and for any x value between 3 and 9, $f(x) > 0$.

370. (B) If $ax - b = 0$, then $ax = b$ and $x = \dfrac{b}{a}$. Therefore, a and b can have any values where $\dfrac{b}{a} = -7$. Of the pairs of values given, you need a pair where b is 7 or -7 and a has the opposite sign; only choice B meets these conditions.

371. (B) The equation crosses the x-axis at one point, so there will be one real solution to $f(x) = 0$.

372. (C) Using the table, $f(2) = 8$. Therefore, $\dfrac{f(2)}{4} = \dfrac{8}{4} = 2 = 12x$, so $x = \dfrac{2}{12}$, or $\dfrac{1}{6}$.

373. (E) Setting the equations equal to each other, $2x^2 + 14 = x^2 + 30$. Collecting terms gives us $x^2 = 16$. This equation has solutions $x = 4$, $x = -4$. But since $a < 0$, we will use $x = -4$. At $x = -4$, $b = f(-4) = 2(16) + 14 = 46$.

374. (D) $s(4) = -4^2 + 9(4) = -16 + 36 = 20$

375. (D) Since the coefficient on the first term is positive, the graph of the function is a parabola opening up. Additionally, since $x^2 - 9x + 8 = (x - 8)(x - 1)$, the function crosses the x-axis at $x = 8$ and $x = 1$. Therefore, for values of x between 1 and 8, $f(x)$ will be negative.

376. (B) The given equation is equivalent to $x^3 = \dfrac{9}{2}$, which has one solution, $x = \sqrt[3]{\dfrac{9}{2}}$.

377. (B) While there may be more zeros, there must be at least two, since the table shows two instances where $g(x) = 0$.

378. (E) If n is larger than m^2, the expression will be negative. Otherwise, as long as m^2 is larger than $n + 3$, the expression will be positive.

379. (B) The equation $-x^2 - 15 = 0$ is equivalent to the equation $x^2 = -15$, which has no real solutions.

380. (C) The graph of the function $f(x)$ moved up 10 units will be represented by the function $f(x) + 10$. This means every y-coordinate will be increased by 10 units.

381. (D) Substituting 3 in each of the expressions in the answer choices, we find that $10(3) - 10 = 30 - 10 = 20$.

382. (D) $\dfrac{g(x)}{f(x)} = \dfrac{x^2 - x - 6}{x + 2} = \dfrac{(x-3)(x+2)}{x+2} = x - 3, x \neq -2$

383. (D) $x^2 + 2x + 1 = (x+1)^2$, which has a single root of $x = -1$

384. (A) If $f(b) = 18$, then $2b + 6 = 18$, and $2b = 12$. Therefore, $b = \dfrac{12}{2} = 6$.

385. (E) The equation $x^2 = 8x - 15$ is equivalent to $x^2 - 8x + 15 = 0$, or $(x - 3)(x - 5) = 0$. The possible values of x are then solutions to the equations $x - 3 = 0$ and $x - 5 = 0$; those solutions are $x = 3$ and $x = 5$.

Chapter 7

386. (B) To find the width of the track, take the outer radius of the curve and subtract the inner radius: $44m - 37m = 7m$. Since there are 6 lanes in the track, divide 7 meters by 6 to get 1.2 meters per lane.

387. (D) First, find the total area enclosed including the track and the grassy area. This includes the two semicircles (forming a whole circle) and the rectangle between them:

$$\pi r_{outer}^{\,2} + lw = 3.14159(44^2) + 84(88) = 13,474 m^2$$

Next find the total sodded area within the track:

$$\pi r_{inner}^{\,2} + lw = 3.14159(37^2) + 84(74) = 10,517 m^2$$

To find the paved area of the track only, subtract the two values:

$$13474 m^2 - 10517 m^2 = 2957 m^2$$

The cost for the asphalt on the paved area is $20 per square meter, so the asphalt cost is:

$2957 m^2 \left(\dfrac{\$20}{1\ m^2} \right) = \$59,143$. The cost for the sod is $4 per square meter, so the sod cost is:

$10517 m^2 \left(\dfrac{\$4}{1\ m^2} \right) = \$42,068$. Thus, the total project cost is $59,143 + $42,068 = $101,211,

which rounds to $101,000.

388. (C) Since the area is 16 and $ABCD$ is a square, $AD = CD = 4$, and $\tan x = \dfrac{4}{4} = 1$.

389. (B) Using the midpoint formula, $M = \left(\dfrac{2+5}{2}, \dfrac{7+7}{2} \right) = \left(\dfrac{7}{2}, 7 \right)$.

390. (E) If M is the midpoint, the length of AM will be $\sqrt{(2-1)^2 + (5-0)^2} = \sqrt{1+25} = \sqrt{26}$. Since M is the midpoint, this is half the length of the line AB.

391. (A) The point where the line crosses the y-axis is the y-intercept and can be found by putting the line in slope-intercept form (solving for y). This is written as $y = mx + b$, with m as the slope and b as the y-intercept. The resulting equation is $y = -10 + 7x$, and $b = -10$.

392. (D) Since R is the midpoint of QP, the length of QP is $2(6) = 12$. Further, since MQ has a length of 4, MP has a length of $12 + 4 = 16$. Finally, P is the midpoint of MN, so the length of MN is $16 \times 2 = 32$.

393. (E) Since m and n are parallel, the sum of angles x and y must be 180, and since x is 36, $y = 180 - 36 = 144$.

394. (B) Quite often on a geometry question with no figures given, it helps if you make a quick sketch. Plotting out points A, B, and C should give you a clear idea of where point D must be. Since the figure is a rectangle, point D will have the same x-coordinate as point A and the same y-coordinate as point C. This leads to the answer of $(1, 6)$.

395. (C) Using the slope formula, $m = \dfrac{\frac{1}{4} - 2}{-\frac{1}{4} - \left(-\frac{1}{2}\right)} = \dfrac{\frac{1}{4} - \frac{8}{4}}{-\frac{1}{4} + \frac{2}{4}} = \dfrac{-\frac{7}{4}}{\frac{1}{4}} = -7$.

396. (E) Let h be the height of triangle ABC. Given the area, $\frac{1}{2}(5)h = 50$, and $h = 20$. For triangle MNP, the area is $\frac{1}{2}(5)(20 + 10) = 75$.

397. (C) In the triangle with two 60-degree angles, the missing angle is $180 - 120 = 60$ degrees. In the triangle with two angles of 85 degrees, the missing angle is $180 - 170 = 10$ degrees. Since the central angle of any circle has a measure of 360 degrees, the angle AOB is $360 - 60 - 10 - 115 = 175$ degrees.

398. (E) The slope of a line in the form $ax + by = c$ is $-(\frac{a}{b})$. In this case, the slope is $\frac{5}{2}$, and any line perpendicular to this line will have a slope of $-\frac{2}{5}$. Only the equation in choice E satisfies this condition.

399. (C) Using the point-slope formula, $y - 5 = -\frac{5}{4}(x - (-3))$. This equation simplifies to $y = -\frac{5}{4}x + \frac{5}{4}$.

400. (E) With a negative slope, the line will fall from left to right. Starting with the positive y-intercept, this leaves the only possibility for an x-intercept as being along the positive x-axis.

401. (E) The line PQ is parallel to the x-axis. Therefore, the y-coordinates of P and Q must be the same. Since the length of the line is 5, the x-coordinate is $3 + 5 = 8$.

402. (B) The point M is in the second quadrant, where x values are negative and y values are positive. Only choice B satisfies those conditions.

403. (D) Because lines m and n are parallel, angles x and y must have the same value; that is, $x = y$. So $x + y = x + x = 2x = 160$, and $x = 80$. The angles x and z must have a sum of 180, so $z = 100$.

404. (B) If the radius is 6, then the center of the circle is 6 units away from all points on the circumference. The points $(-3, 0)$ and $(-15, 0)$ are both 6 units away from $(-9, 0)$ along the x-axis.

405. (C) Let w be the width of the rectangle and l be the length. We are given that $\tan x = \frac{8}{3} = \frac{l}{AE}$. Since the figure shows that $l = 8$, AE must equal 3. From the figure, $w = AE + 2$; substituting AE from the solution to $\tan x$, $3 + 2 = 5$. The area is thus $w \times l = 5 \times 8 = 40$.

406. (E)

$$-2x + 6y = 14$$
$$-2x + 2x + 6y = 14 + 2x$$
$$6y = 2x + 14$$
$$6y/6 = 2x/6 + 14/6$$
$$y = 1/3 \ x + 7/3$$

407. (B) The process described can be written as $y = 3x + 2$ for an x-coordinate of x. This equation is in slope-intercept form, so it indicates that the resulting line would have a y-intercept of 2.

408. (D) The x-intercept is the point where $y = 0$. In this case, $2x - 5(0) = 10$, and $x = \dfrac{10}{2} = 5$.

409. (D) Any line of the form $x = c$ is parallel to the y-axis, which is equivalent to being perpendicular to the x-axis. The x-intercept is c, but there is no y-intercept because the line is parallel to the y-axis, so III is not true.

410. (B) Using the slope formula,

$$0 - 9/3 - 0 = -9/3 = -3$$

411. (D) The length of line PM is $4 - (-1) = 5$. Since M is the midpoint of PQ, the length of MQ must also be 5. Therefore, $x - 4 = 5$, and $x = 9$.

412. (B) Solving the given equation for $x = 2$, $14 - 6y = 8$, and $y = 1$.

413. (A) Since ABC is an equilateral triangle, each side must have a length of 3. The distance between the points in answer choice A is 3, as the difference along the x-axis between $(-3, 2)$ and $(0, 2)$ would be 3.

414. (C) Given that the point $(4, y)$ is on the line, solving the given equation for $x = 4$ will give us the value of y. This yields the equation $-32 - 4y = 16$, which has a solution $y = -12$.

415. (D) In a parallelogram, opposite angles are congruent. Here, $x = 125$, and $y = 55$.

416. (A) The triangle is a 30-60-90 triangle, which always has legs x (opposite the 30-degree angle) and $x\sqrt{3}$ (opposite the 60-degree angle), along with a hypotenuse of $2x$. Since the hypotenuse here is 8, $x = 4$, and this is equal to the length of the side opposite the 30-degree angle.

417. (E) If the midpoint of line AB is on the y-axis, then the distance from A to the y-axis must be the same as the distance from B to the y-axis. Additionally, since the line must be perpendicular to the y-axis, the y-coordinate of the two points will be the same. The point A is 8 units from the y-axis, so the point B must be as well.

418. (C) The lines will intersect where $y = 8$. Substitute this value of y into the given equation: $8 = \dfrac{3}{2}x + 1$, which can be simplified to $7 = \dfrac{3}{2}x$. To solve for x, multiply both sides by $\dfrac{2}{3}$: $x = \dfrac{2}{3}(7) = \dfrac{14}{3}$.

419. (A) The slope of the line passing through the given points is $\dfrac{8-4}{3-(-1)} = \dfrac{4}{4} = 1$. Any line parallel to this line will also have a slope of 1. The answer choices are of the form $y = mx + b$, so the coefficient of x will be the slope. The only equation in which the coefficient of x is 1 is answer choice A.

420. (B) The area of a rhombus is $\dfrac{a \times b}{2}$, where a and b are the diagonals. In this case, the diagonals are m and $2m$, so substitute to solve for the area: $\dfrac{m \times 2m}{2} = \dfrac{2m^2}{2} = m^2$.

421. (D) In all of the equations except answer choice D, y and x are by themselves with an exponent of 1. In answer choice D, the exponent of x is 2 when the expression $x(x + 1)$ is multiplied.

422. (E) Since N is the midpoint of MP, then $MN = NP$ and therefore $14 = 2x$. From this, you can determine that $x = 7$. This can be used to figure out the length of PQ, since $PQ = 4x - 9 = 4(7) - 9 = 28 - 9 = 19$. While 19 is an answer, the question is asking for the length of MQ, not just PQ, so you have to find:

$$MN + NP + PQ = MQ$$
$$14 + 14 + 19 = 47$$

423. (A) Using $x = 2m$ and $y = m - 1$, substitute for x and y in the equation of the line: $m - 1 = 2m + 4$, so $m = -5$.

424. (B) We are given the point $y = \dfrac{x-1}{4} = \dfrac{x}{4} - \dfrac{1}{4} = \dfrac{1}{4}x - \dfrac{1}{4}$. To put the equation in standard form, multiply both sides by 4, and bring the x and y terms to the same side: $4y - x = -1$.

425. (B) To find the answer, you can use the distance formula for two points and then divide by two, since the question states that the distance being looked for is half the distance between P and Q. Placing the values of P and Q into this formula yields

$$\dfrac{\sqrt{(-8-(-4))^2 + (1-2)^2}}{2} = \dfrac{\sqrt{(-4)^2 + (-1)^2}}{2} = \dfrac{\sqrt{17}}{2}.$$

426. (B) The line passes through the points $(1, 0)$ and $(0, 2)$, so the slope is $\dfrac{2-0}{0-1} = -2$.

427. (C) Solving for y, this equation is $y = \frac{1}{2}x + 4$, and any point along this line must have the form $\left(x, \frac{1}{2}x + 4\right)$. Only the point $(0, 4)$ is of this form.

428. (A) The line marked "s" is the hypotenuse of a right triangle formed by the height of the pyramid (147 m) and half the length of the base of the pyramid ($230 \div 2 = 115$ m). Using the Pythagorean theorem to find the length: $s = \sqrt{147^2 + 115^2} = 187$ m.

429. (E) The base of each triangular surface is 230 meters and the height of each triangular surface is 187 meters as calculated in the previous question. The area of one of the triangular surfaces is $\frac{1}{2}bh = \frac{1}{2}(230)(187) = 21,505$ m^2. The limestone covers all four triangular surfaces, so the total are of coverage is $4(21,505$ m$^2) = 86,020$ m^2. Each 40-ton limestone cube covers $(3$ m$)(4$ m$) = 12$ m^2, so the total weight of all the limestones is $86,020$ m$^2\left(\frac{40 \text{ tons}}{12 \text{ m}^2}\right) = 286,733$ tons $\approx 287,000$ tons.

430. (C) To find the point that is on both lines, set the two equations equal: $5x - 1 = -3x - 17$. Collecting terms, $8x = -16$, and $x = -2$. Therefore, the equations intersect at the point with x-coordinate -2. Only answer choice C has this value for the x-coordinate.

431. (C) The radius is the distance from the center of the circle to any point on the circumference. Here, that distance is $\sqrt{(4-2)^2 + (9-5)^2} = \sqrt{4+16} = \sqrt{20} = 2\sqrt{5}$.

432. (A) By definition, $\sin x = \frac{\text{opposite}}{\text{hypotenuse}}$, where "opposite" means the length of the side opposite the angle and "hypotenuse" is the length of the hypotenuse. Here, $\sin x = \frac{9}{15} = \frac{3}{5}$.

433. (E) For all angles, $\sec \alpha = \frac{1}{\cos \alpha}$.

434. (C) To find the area, we must first find the height of the triangle. If we draw the triangle and draw a line from its apex to the base, we will form a right triangle with sides of 6, 3, and h, where h is the height. Using the Pythagorean theorem, $3^2 + h^2 = 6^2$, so $h = \sqrt{36-9} = \sqrt{27} = 3\sqrt{3}$. Now use the formula for the area of the triangle: $A = \frac{1}{2}bh = \frac{1}{2}(6)(3\sqrt{3}) = 9\sqrt{3}$.

435. (C) Using the definition of sine as the opposite side divided by the hypotenuse, $\sin B = \frac{3}{4} = \frac{x}{12}$. Cross multiplying yields the equation $36 = 4x$, so $x = 9$.

436. (C) Using the formula for the area of a circle, $\dfrac{29\pi}{4} = \pi r^2$, so $r = \sqrt{\dfrac{29}{4}} = \dfrac{\sqrt{29}}{2}$. The hypotenuse of the triangle ABC is also the diameter of the circle, which is $2r = \sqrt{29}$. Therefore, by the Pythagorean theorem, $(\sqrt{29})^2 = 2^2 + (BC)^2$, and $BC = 5$. Finally, the area of the triangle is $\dfrac{1}{2}(2)(5) = 5$.

437. (A) The standard form of the equation of a circle is $(x - h)^2 + (y - k)^2 = r^2$, where (h, k) is the center and r is the radius. Using the given values, the equation of this circle is $(x - 0)^2 + (y - (-5))^2 = 2^2$. The first term can be simplified to x^2, and the second term to $(y + 5)^2$.

438. (D) If the legs have lengths 2 and 4, then the hypotenuse has a length of $\sqrt{2^2 + 4^2} = \sqrt{20} = 2\sqrt{5}$.

439. (E) If the length of the smaller leg is x, then the larger leg is $3x$, and by the Pythagorean theorem, the hypotenuse is $\sqrt{x^2 + 9x^2} = x\sqrt{10} = 10$, the given length. Solving for x, $x = \dfrac{10}{\sqrt{10}} = \dfrac{10\sqrt{10}}{10} = \sqrt{10}$, and the perimeter is $\sqrt{10} + 3\sqrt{10} + 10$.

440. (C) The circumference of any circle is $2\pi r$, where r is the radius.

441. (A) The cosine of x is the ratio of the lengths of the side adjacent to the angle and the hypotenuse. Here, those sides have lengths b and a, respectively.

442. (A) The formula of a circle in the (x, y) coordinate plane is $(x - h)^2 + (y - k)^2 = r^2$, where (h, k) is the center and r is the radius. The line AB is a diameter with a length of 10 (which can be found by looking at the y-coordinates of A and B), so the radius must be 5. Further, the center will occur at the halfway point along the line, which is $(6, 5)$.

443. (E) The diagonal AC is also the diameter of the circle, which we can use to find the radius and thus the area. In a square, the diagonal and two sides form a 45-45-90 triangle with sides x, x, and $x\sqrt{2}$. Therefore, the diameter of the circle is $3\sqrt{2}$, and the radius is $\dfrac{3\sqrt{2}}{2}$. Using the area formula for a circle, $A = \pi \left(\dfrac{3\sqrt{2}}{2} \right)^2 = \pi \left(\dfrac{9(2)}{4} \right) = \pi \left(\dfrac{9}{2} \right) = \dfrac{9\pi}{2}$.

444. (E) By the Pythagorean theorem, the hypotenuse will have a length of $\sqrt{(5x)^2 + x^2} = \sqrt{26x^2} = x\sqrt{26}$.

445. (A) The area is the base (9) times the height, which is unknown. The height is a leg of the right triangle with a hypotenuse of 5 and a second leg of 1. Therefore, by the Pythagorean theorem, $1^2 + h^2 = 5^2$, where h is the unknown height. Solving for h, $h = \sqrt{24} = 2\sqrt{6}$, and the area of the parallelogram is $9(2\sqrt{6}) = 18\sqrt{6}$.

446. (C) Because ABC is an equilateral triangle, each of its interior angles has a measure of 60 degrees. The angle at point C has been split into two angles; one has a measure of 20 degrees, so the other has a measure of $60 - 20 = 40$ degrees. Finally, the triangle containing the angle labeled x has interior angles of 40 degrees and 60 degrees, so $x = 180 - 40 - 60 = 80$.

447. (B) Using the standard form of the equation of a circle, $(x - h)^2 + (y - k)^2 = r^2$, you can determine that the radius of the circle is 2, and the center is at the point (8, 10). Any point exactly two units from (8, 10) will lie on the circumference of the circle. You can then use the distance formula between two points to determine the answer is B.

448. (D) Given that $\tan x = \dfrac{1}{2} = \dfrac{\text{opposite}}{\text{adjacent}}$ and $h =$ the length of the hypotenuse, then $h^2 = 1^2 + 2^2$, and $h = \sqrt{5}$. Therefore, $\sin x = \dfrac{\text{opposite}}{\text{hypotenuse}} = \dfrac{1}{\sqrt{5}} = \dfrac{\sqrt{5}}{5}$.

449. (D) Let r represent the radius of a circle. Using the formula for circumference, the given inequality is $2\pi r > x$. Solving for r, $r > \dfrac{x}{2\pi}$.

450. (B) Using the formula for circumference and dividing by 2 because this is a half circle, arc $PQ = \dfrac{1}{2}(2\pi(2)) = 2\pi$.

Chapter 8

451. (B) The number of students with blue or green eyes is $16 + 4 = 20$ students. The probability of selecting one of these 20 students from a population of 200 total students is $\dfrac{20}{200} = \dfrac{10}{100} = \dfrac{1}{10}$.

452. (D) If h hazel-eyed students are added to the original hazel-eyed population of 24 students and the original total population of 200, the new probability of selecting a hazel-eyed student from the population is $\dfrac{24 + h}{200 + h}$. Setting this equal to the new $\dfrac{1}{2}$ probability, h may be solved for as follows: $\dfrac{24 + h}{200 + h} = \dfrac{1}{2}$. Cross multiplying: $2(24 + h) = 1(200 + h)$. This yields: $48 + 2h = 200 + h$, for which $h = 152$.

453. (D) Without the brown-eyed students, the new population size is $200 - 110 = 90$ students. With only 24 hazel-eyed students in the population, the probability of selecting a hazel-eyed student is $\dfrac{24}{90} = \dfrac{12}{45} = \dfrac{4}{15}$.

454. (E) The probability of rolling a 5 on the first roll is $\frac{1}{6}$. The probability of rolling a 6 on the second roll is also $\frac{1}{6}$. The probability of rolling a 5 and then a 6 is the product of both these probabilities: $\left(\frac{1}{6}\right) \cdot \left(\frac{1}{6}\right) = \frac{1}{36}$.

455. (D) To calculate the number of students in the junior class taking the ACT, take 60% of 250, which is 150 students. Since only half of these students took the essay portion of the test, then 75 students took the essay portion of the ACT.

456. (E) To find the total number of shirt/pants combinations, multiply 5 and 3 to get 15 combinations. Each of these combinations may be paired with two pairs of shoes, yielding 30 total outfits possible.

457. (D) To calculate an average, take the sum of all the students' scores divided by the number of students. For each class, the sum of all their scores may be calculated as follows: $\frac{Sum\ of\ Class\ 1's\ scores}{20} = 0.82$. *Sum of Class 1's scores* $= (20)0.8 = 16.4$. Also, $\frac{Sum\ of\ Class\ 2's\ scores}{26} = 0.86$. Sum of Class 2's scores $= (26)0.86 = 22.36$. To calculate the combined classes average: $\frac{Sum\ of\ Class\ 1's\ scores + Sum\ of\ Class\ 2's\ scores}{Total\ \#\ of\ students\ in\ both\ classes} =$

$\frac{16.4 + 22.36}{20 + 26} = 0.843 = 84.3\%$.

458. (C) There are a total of 15 cards, and 6 are blue. Therefore, the probability will be $\frac{6}{15} = \frac{2}{5}$.

459. (A) The ratio of the first term to the second term is $\frac{2}{3}$. Likewise, the ratio of the second to the third term is $\frac{3}{\left(\frac{9}{2}\right)} = \frac{2}{3}$. If the fourth term in the series is x, then the ratio of the third term to the fourth term can be found from $\frac{\left(\frac{9}{2}\right)}{x} = \frac{2}{3}$. Cross multiplying gives $3\left(\frac{9}{2}\right) = 2x$. Solving this for x yields $\frac{27}{4}$.

460. (B) If $x = 2y$, then $\frac{1}{2}x = y$ and $\frac{x+y}{2} = \frac{x + \frac{1}{2}x}{2} = \frac{\frac{3}{2}x}{2} = \frac{3}{4}x = 30$. Solving this equation yields the solution $x = 40$.

461. (D) By the multiplication rule, the number of different combinations will be $3 \times 2 \times 8 = 48$.

462. (C) With a pair of 6-sided die rolled together, there are $(6)(6) = 36$ possible outcomes. Since they are rolled together, there are two ways to get a 5/6 combination. Either the first is a 5 and the second is a 6, or the first is a 6 and the second is a 5. So there are two combinations out of 36 possible outcomes, giving a probability of $\dfrac{2}{36} = \dfrac{1}{18}$.

463. (B) Let B represent the number of blue pens. Then the total number of pens is $B + 2B = 3B$, and the probability of selecting a blue pen is $\dfrac{B}{3B} = \dfrac{1}{3}$.

464. (B) The bag must contain $\dfrac{4}{5}(110) = 88$ green marbles and $110 - 88 = 22$ marbles that are not green.

465. (E) The probability of any event is always between zero and one inclusive. Additionally, the probability of event A occurring is always equal to one minus the probability of the event not occurring (also called the complementary event).

466. (B) The average is found by taking the total of the values and dividing by how many values there are. In this case, we would have an average of $\dfrac{m}{n} = p$, which simplifies to $np = m$. Next, to write n in terms of m and p, divide both sides by p to get $n = \dfrac{m}{p}$.

467. (B) Arithmetic sequences are formed when each number in the sequence is the sum of some fixed number and the number before it. Suppose the fixed number being added to every term is x. Then for us to get from the second term to the tenth term, x must have been added to eight terms. Expressed as an equation, $6 + 8x = 38$, so $8x = 32$. This equation has a solution of $x = 4$. Finally, because the second term was found by adding 4 to the first term, the first term must have been $6 - 4 = 2$.

468. (C) By the multiplication rule, there are $4 \times 3 \times 2 \times 1$ ways to arrange the letters.

469. (E) Coin flips are independent of each other. Although the flips so far have resulted in tails, the probability that a fair coin will land on tails in an individual flip is always $\dfrac{1}{2}$.

470. (E) Since the sequence repeats every 6 numbers, the 6th, 12th, 18th, 24th, and 30th numbers in the sequence will be 2. Therefore, the next 5 terms will be $-1, 5, -2, 1, 5$.

471. (C) Out of the total of 25 numbers between 1 and 25, there are 9 prime numbers (2, 3, 5, 7, 11, 13, 17, 19, and 23).

472. (A) The lower the probability, the less likely an event is to occur.

473. (B) After the first entry is drawn, only 6 are left. One of these entries is Sara's, giving a probability of $\dfrac{1}{6}$ it will be selected.

474. (E) By the multiplication rule, he has $5 \times 4 \times 10$ complete sets.

475. (B) Let x represent the sum of the six numbers. Then, since the average is 10, $\frac{x}{6} = 10$, and $x = 60$. When 5 is added to each number in the set, the new average is $\frac{60 + (6 \times 5)}{6} = \frac{90}{6} = 15$.

476. (E) Since it is not possible to choose both Hanna and Jake, the probability of one or the other being chosen is the sum of the probabilities of each of them being chosen individually: $\frac{1}{29} + \frac{1}{29} = \frac{2}{29}$.

477. (D) The probability of an event not occurring is one minus the probability it will occur. Here, $P(\text{not even}) = 1 - P(\text{even}) = 1 - \frac{1}{m} = \frac{m}{m} - \frac{1}{m} = \frac{m-1}{m}$.

478. (C) When two 6-sided die are rolled, there are $(6)(6) = 36$ possible outcomes. The only way to roll a combined score of three is if the first dice is a 1 and the second is a 2, or if the first dice is a 2 and the second is a 1. So the total probability is $\frac{2}{36} = \frac{1}{18}$.

479. (D) By the multiplication rule and the fact that a person cannot hold two positions, the total is $30 \times 29 \times 28$.

480. (A) The average of any set of numbers is the sum of those numbers divided by how many numbers are in the set.

481. (B) In the initial shipment of eight phones, five are not defective. After one good phone is removed, there are seven total phones, four of which are not defective.

482. (A) Increasing the number of green marbles would decrease the probability of selecting a white marble, and decreasing both by the same number would also decrease the probability of selecting a white marble because since there are fewer white marbles, the number removed would represent a larger proportion of the white marbles.

483. (A) If the probability is three times as large, the number of the first type must be three times the number of the second type. Therefore, the box must contain $\frac{240}{3}$ coins of the second type.

484. (D) The median is the middle number when the numbers in the list are placed in order. Since there are seven numbers in the original list, 3 must be the fourth number when the list is placed in order. When the new number is added, the new median will be the average of the fourth and fifth numbers. The numbers are distinct, so the fifth number must be larger than 3, and the median will therefore also be larger than 3.

485. (D) By the multiplication rule, there are $5 \times 4 \times 3 \times 2$ ways to arrange four of these letters.

486. (E) Given that $x = 7$, the set can be written as $\{2, 18, -7, 12, 10\}$, which contains four even numbers. Since there are a total of five numbers in the set, the probability of selecting an even number is $\frac{4}{5}$.

487. (C) If x is the median, it must be in the middle of the list when the items are placed in order. This means two numbers must be smaller than x, and since z and y are larger than 4, the smaller numbers must be 1 and 4. Given this information, the correct order of the list would be 1, 4, x, z, y, and only the inequality in answer choice C holds.

488. (D) Given this schedule, Aiden will work 16 (or 4×4) of the 28 (or 7×4) days.

489. (D) By the multiplication rule, there are $5 \times 3 = 15$ choices.

490. (D) Let x be the smallest of the integers. The remaining integers are therefore $x + 1$, $x + 2$, and $x + 3$. Given the average, we can say that $\frac{x + (x+1) + (x+2) + (x+3)}{4} = 14.5$, which is equivalent to $\frac{4x + 6}{4} = 14.5$. Therefore, $x + \frac{3}{2} = 14.5$, or $x = 13$. This means the largest integer is $13 + 3 = 16$, and the sum of x and $x + 3$ is $13 + 16 = 29$.

491. (E) The probability of an event not occurring is 1 minus the probability of the event occurring. Therefore, probability I is 0.6, and probability II is 0.8. Finally, if both events cannot occur at the same time, the probability that one or the other will occur is the sum of their individual probabilities. Thus, probability III is $0.4 + 0.2 = 0.6$. All of these probabilities are greater than 0.5.

492. (D) Since only red and black cards are in the box, the probability of selecting a red card or a black card must have a sum of 1. If x is the probability of selecting a black card, then $\frac{1}{2}x$ is the probability of selecting a red card, and $x + \frac{1}{2}x = \frac{3}{2}x = 1$. Therefore, $x = \frac{2}{3}$.

493. (D) The probability of any event occurring must be smaller than or equal to 1.

494. (C) The total of all the probabilities must be 1, since the events represent all possible choices: $1 - \frac{2}{5} - \frac{1}{8} = \frac{40}{40} - \frac{16}{40} - \frac{5}{40} = \frac{19}{40}$.

495. (E) The median is the middle value if the list items are put in order from smallest to largest. Using the inequality, w would be the middle number of the data list.

496. (D) Since the list has an even number of values, the median is the average of x and y: $\frac{x + y}{2} = 5$, and the sum of x and y must be 10. Therefore, the product of x and y must be the product of two numbers that add up to 10. Only answer choice D satisfies this property.

497. (B) Given that the probability an item is not on sale at a discount is $\dfrac{2}{3}$, then there must be $\dfrac{2}{3} \times 171 = 114$ items not on sale at a discount and $171 - 114 = 57$ items on sale at a discount.

498. (C) There are 5 biology books of 35 total books, so the probability is $\dfrac{5}{35} = \dfrac{1}{7}$.

499. (D) The total number of students in the group is $82 + 18 + 22 + 48 + 30 = 200$. Of these, 18 indicated interest in an aviation career, so the probability is $\dfrac{18}{200} = \dfrac{9}{100}$.

500. (B) Hats in the bin are either black or gray. Therefore, the probability of selecting a gray hat and the probability of selecting a black hat must total 1. In other words, $P(\text{gray}) + P(\text{black}) = 1$, so $P(\text{black}) = 1 - P(\text{gray}) = 1 - x$.

NOTES